NEW INFORMATION TECHNOLOGY AND WOMEN

NEW INFORMATION TECHNOLOGY AND WOMEN

D N Prasad

MD PUBLICATIONS PVT LTD
NEW DELHI
www.mdppl.com

Published by :

MD Publications Pvt Ltd
"MD House", 11, Darya Ganj,
New Delhi - 110 002
Phone : +91-11-45355555
E-mail : contact@mdppl.com
Website: www.mdppl.com

ISBN: 978-81-7533-360-4

Published and Printed by Mr. Pranav Gupta on behalf of **MD Publications Pvt Ltd** at Times Press, Delhi.

PREFACE

Global concerns about current and future roles of women in computing occupations gained more importance with the emerging information age. These concerns motivated public policy debates addressing gender equality as computer applications exerted increasing influence in society. This dialog helped to expand information technology innovations and to reduce the unintended consequences of perceived sexism.

A proposal from an economical standpoint suggests that in order to avert the computing and IT industry from dangers such as global sourcing, a solution is needed to increase the participation of underrepresented groups like women. It has also been claimed that there is a growing demand for IT workers with leadership, interpersonal, and communication skills in order to combat the general drop in worker retention and ineffective training. In particular, the cost of replacing a skilled technical employee has been estimated to be as high as 120% of the yearly salary of the position.

On a similar note, it has been argued that the inclusion of women in computing will mitigate innovation-hindering effects such as groupthink by preventing the group from becoming too homogenized. Gender diversity has been suggested to give benefits such as better decision making, increased creativity, and enhanced, innovative performances. The situation in Asian countries differs greatly. Research suggests that Malaysia has a much more equal split that varies around the half-way mark. It is suggested that this may be due to the fact that Malaysian women view careers in IT as a means of employment rather than a status symbol. A job in the Computing industry also implies a safe work environment.

In India, the case is just the opposite of that in the western countries. There is a great demand for computer science, but not enough reputed colleges which offer quality education. Since the IT industry has been responsible for large-scale employment, there is a higher rate of women taking up education and careers in engineering, especially computer engineering. Computer engineering is a relatively clean field in the sense that it does not involve careers in factories. Most careers are in programming, which can be easily done from home too.

But, bearing in mind the lack of generalizable evidence, it does appear that the likely impact of IT on women, and the role they are playing in the IT area, may be minimal, considering the general status of women in African societies and their position in the technical fields. With the increased penetration of computers in organizations, both in the public and private sectors in Africa, there must have been some impact, however small, positive or negative, on women.

I am very grateful to Mr. Pranav Gupta, Director of MD Publications Pvt Ltd, New Delhi, for his kind cooperation and support for this book.

D N Prasad

Contents

1

New World of Information Technology

Issues of safety and security will require organizations to introduce new job classification for the Information Ranger. As the workgroup replaces the work group, organizations must reinvest some of the productivity gains in the organization to compensate employees for the loss of opportunities to interact with each other. The new technology can help managers deal with issues of control, coordination, and the needs of the special employees. However, administrators must recognize that some affects of the information technology can be dysfunctional.

Advances in information technology influence the proliferation of new devices for handling, entering, retrieving and manipulating data. With the help of new products it is possible for managers to accommodate employees that are home-bound or prefer to work at home. For example, software such as AT&T's "The Home Agent" automatically redirects calls to allow telecommuters, employees that work at home, to answer telephone calls as if they were at the office. Taking advantage of such capabilities administrators can save resources that would otherwise be consumed to underwrite the direct and indirect costs of office space such as rent, parking, or security.

The emerging computer technology will allow managers to do all of the above while improving service quality and enhancing responsiveness to the public. Taking advantage of the new hardware and software supervisors will be able to augment equity in dealing with subordinates and service recipients. However, the new technology can be dysfunctional.

While some of the dysfunctional capabilities are inherent to the technology, others may result when managers fail to understand the need for corrective actions. The intention of this chapter is to help managers avoid some undesired experiences by pointing out how the new technology can change group dynamics. The article also asserts that managers must be aware of the possible implications of the new technology for issues of safety and security as well as the new possibilities for dealing with the employee with special needs.

Changes in information technology should be followed by a corresponding change in structure and management practices. Yet, many administrators are slow to comprehend the implications of various hardware and software capabilities for carrying out the mission of their units. This tendency is augmented in the case of individuals who do not keep up with professional readings. Without the regular scanning of professional journals and computer magazines, grasping intuitively the meaning of the terminology used to describe new hardware and software, e.g., GUI, MIPS, OP, OCR, MINA, SQL etc. is impossible.

As we move into the mid 1990s the theoretical capabilities of new hardware and software seem to determine the bench mark against which the productivity of agencies will be measured. Consequently, public administrators will experience a mounting pressure to take advantage of the most recent developments in information technology as they become available or risk an accusation that they are ineffective or unresponsive. Because of the rapid changes and accelerated proliferation of products that use the latest technology in the private sector, government agencies must absorb and adapt to new hardware and software to keep pace with developments in the industries they regulate or the various needs of the publics they serve.

Yet, without knowing the possible implications of the new information technology for the human side of the enterprise, administrators may find their effort counterproductive. Following the investment in hardware and software, they may discover that they need to deal with new and more, not fewer, problems of performance and morale. One reason for such dysfunctional results is that changes in information technology render the experiences of many employees (or agency clientele) irrelevant for the task at hand.

A case in point involves building permits in New York City. Under the headline "Computer Slowing the Pace of Permits" The New York Times reports that service recipients "say it used to take an average of a week to 10 days from the initial filing of an application... until a building permit was issued. Since the computer was installed, they contend, it takes three to six weeks". Now, besides the regular problems of running the Building Department in Manhattan, managers must deal with new complaints from the public, media inquiries, and employees that are stressed because they need to adjust to a new system while dealing with an angrier clientele.

One goal of this chapter is not only to alert managers about implications of new information technology for supervisors but to review some of the ramifications for human resource management (HRM). The chapter starts by examining how the new technology influences issues of safety and security. It suggests that organizations should look for and deal expediently with threats to the integrity of their operation or risks to the health or welfare of employees that use the new technology. It points out that in order to deal with complex security-and-safety issues, organizations will have to develop a new classification of expert employees with multi-disciplinary backgrounds or experiences. The chapter refers to these experts as Information Rangers to denote the combination of policing and investigative authority with specialized knowledge and survival skills.

With the new information technology, importing and exporting data becomes a function of hardware and software compatibility rather than group dynamics. In the past, work groups developed when employees pursued the same task, dealt with the same client, reported to a common supervisor or utilized common resources. In the future, some work groups (which are natural groups and social entities) will be replaced by workgroups that are devoid of a social or psychological function.

This chapter explores the characteristics of the workgroup, the artificial entity that results from the use of common information resources. It looks at some differences between work group and workgroup and the possible implications for managers and productivity. The discussion suggests that the benefits of the new technology are not without cost. In order to minimize the cost, organizations should take an affirmative action to provide employees with new and more opportunities to socialize and to develop interpersonal relations. The purpose of such activities is to restore the social context of work that is being eroded when face to face interactions are replaced by electronic mail (E-Mail) and bulletin boards (BBS).

This chapter suggests that to sustain the productivity that results from the introduction of advanced information technology, managers must invest in the human side of the enterprise. Such investments may indvolve the use of some resources that were saved due to the use of the new technology. It cautions managers of public organizations to avoid the mistakes made by manufacturers in the introduction of robotics and automation.

THE CHALLENGE OF SAFETY AND SECURITY

Noting the failure of government and industry to protect computer security, the National Research Council urged the formation of a privately owned foundation to monitor the problem. This move implies the concern that in addition to possible damage to the business interest of an agency; information technology presents public employees with a new set of legal problems. If they are not careful, public administrators may find themselves involved in litigation concerning possible compromise of individuals' welfare or privacy rights. Such cases are bound to emerge as more of the agency's official and privileged records and information could be accessed from outside its physical quarters.

In a related development, the Computer System Security and Privacy Advisory Board of the National Institute of Standards and Technology (NIST) criticized a bill sponsored by then U.S. Sen. Albert Gore, Jr., that would establish a $1.9 billion program in high performance computing and communications. The board said that the bill did not adequately address security and privacy on the National Research and Education Network (NREN), whose development would be partly funded by the bill. Two recent episodes illustrate the nature of the problem.

The first case is the raiding of Challenger Ltd., a government surplus store, in rural Nancy, Kentucky. The raid in the Fall of 1990 was part of the government's effort to retrieve a broken computer. The computer's hard disk was not erased before it was sold with other broken computers as surplus equipment. The disk contained seven years' worth of documentation from the U.S. Attorney's Office in Lexington, including names of undercover informants, federally protected witnesses, sealed indictments, and other sensitive records.

The owner of Challenger Ltd. refused a government request to supply the names and addresses of computer buyers. This incident confirms the validity of the low score given to federal computer security by the General Accounting Office in its review of the Computer Security Act of 1987. In the second case, a stolen laptop computer could have jeopardized the United Kingdom's Persian Gulf War plans. The computer was stolen from an official military vehicle used to transport a senior aid to the commandant of the British forces in the Gulf. One can only speculate on the cost of the ensuing effort to recover the computer, change the war plans or to deal with criticism and questions after the theft became headline news.

Using computers and software that never leave the office building does not provide immunity from risks like computer viruses or a shelter from legal liability. However, using portable computers or accessing the system from the outside increases such risks. The inter-connectivity of computer networks allowed the Internet worm, the self replicated program, to bring to their knees tens of thousands of network users when a graduate student prank ran amok in November 1988. The incident demonstrated how vulnerable an agency can be after the introduction of new information technology.

Arrangements for providing telecommuters remote access to official data banks and agency reports can enhance productivity. However, this access creates a security risk. Unauthorized parties can use a modem and the same communication protocol for sharing or even manipulating data for their own interests. Protecting the agency from such experiences requires a proactive approach for controlling access to sensitive data. Yet, such efforts are not without a cost and are not full-proof.

Auditors for the Hawaii state tax office in Honolulu use telework centers on a regular basis. These remote work facilities are equipped to allow employees access to their agency's computers by telephone. So far, no public record indicates a security problem due to the new practice. Security considerations cannot be dismissed as insignificant however. A proactive approach by public managers will not prevent all security problems, but it may delay (or prevent) the occurrence of some.

A sensible and cost effective approach to security recognizes the problem before a system fails. In the aftermath of a problem, the cost of added security measures may be very high. An agency may have to use more resources than the amount called for by the nature of the problem it experienced. It will be expected not only to correct the problem but to demonstrate an overall commitment to secure the integrity of data and operations. A proactive approach may allow an agency to spend just the amount for preempting a problem and forego the additional expenses for demonstrating the said commitment.

Another dimension of the security issue has to do with protection of employees who send or receive sensitive information electronically. A leading trade publication of the computer industry observed that "from software-savvy colleagues with the power to decrypt messages to nontechnical co-workers who forward sensitive messages to the boss, a myriad of potential security breaches threatens to compromise the privacy of mail that users send over local area networks (LAN) and public networks." Increasing the security of electronic mail by encryption leads to an increase in processing time and software cost.

Besides snooping by unauthorized co-workers, a very complex issue involves the invasion of privacy versus the rights of management to monitor work related communications and data banks. Sometimes, such monitoring takes place in spite of management promises not to do so. Alana Shoars, a former E-mail administrator at Epson America, is suing her employer. She was fired after confronting her own supervisor about reading E-mail of other employees, contrary to a promise of confidentiality Shoars made to them.

Shoshana Zuboff says: "Data once kept privately have become widely accessible, making an organization visible and transparent in a new way. Yet, some managers' use that visibility to police subordinates instead of to increase employee learning about the business and the markets it serves". In response to employees complaints, the Social Security Administration relaxed some of its eavesdropping practices for workers who take calls from the public. The new policy applies to workers who have been with the agency for more than two years but not for new employees. The Senate Labour Committee's Subcommittee on Employment and Productivity is expected to consider legislation in response to employees' complaints.

Employers contend that electronic monitoring of employees' interaction with callers is necessary for managing complex operations, for quality assurance, and for learning about the need to make adjustment in reaction to changing situations. Such adjustments include reassignment of employees and identification of training needs as well as changes in operational procedures that do not involve the monitored employee. Employers also contend that they have the right to know what employees do on company time or by using company resources.

At the same time, many employers admit that such snooping is used to police the work force. It allows them to identify employees who willfully violate stated policy about proper conduct and interaction with the public or about the misuse of resources such as E-mail, fax, or long distance calls. Common sense suggests that employers should post a warning to employees about possible electronic monitoring. The bragging by a United Parcel Service (UPS) executive that "UPS is unique in putting its privacy statement on its log-on screen" suggests that other executives may not realize that the best interest of the organization is not served by ignoring the rights of the individual employee.

Last, when it comes to issues of safety and security, what is the employer's liability, and what are the implications of an injury that can be related to the use of the new information technology, for the employer and the employee, under the Workers Compensation Act? Who is responsible when an employee does not follow the manufacturer's instructions while operating a government computer, a fax machine, or a copier for other than official business? Who is responsible when a telecommuting employee trips on a computer cord that is used for performing official work? Other liability(s) may occur when the agency provides malfunctioning hardware that causes fire or other physical damage to the employee, members of his/her household, or a third party.

Issues of safety and security cannot be separated from issues of health and the responsibility of the employers to take the necessary precautions. As Jordan sees it "employers who ignore the well being of their computer operators risk lost productivity, labour unrest, increased worker compensation cost, high turn-over" (Jordan 1988). We might expect work-place injuries to become a thing of the past as technology improves and as the number of workers shifts from manufacturing to services. Yet, even though today's automated work place seems much safer, the new information technology brings its own set of health problems.

A case in point is a growing concern about the health of employees who use computer terminals. The clinical data are still inconclusive. However, it seems that static electricity from computer terminals attracts dust particles and pollutes the air that employees breathe. The dangers of Very Low Frequency (VLF) or Extremely Low Frequency (ELF) waves from video display terminals (VDT/CRT) are still under study. Yet there are growing concerns about the health of employees who use computers regularly. In a recent report, the U.S. Environmental Protection Agency (EPA) branded electromagnetic fields (EMF), like the ones generated by computers and VDTs, "a possible human carcinogen".

Uncertainty and concern about the possible effects of prolonged exposure led New York City to pass an ordinance that provides city employees who work near computer terminals with extra breaks. New York City followed the pattern that was established in July 1988 by an ordinance that covered all employees in both public and private offices in Suffolk County (NY). The ordinance did not take effect because the authority of Suffolk County to legislate the behaviour of other government and private employers in the county was challenged in court.

However, in the Fall of 1990 a majority of San Francisco supervisors supported legislation that would require offices with more than 15 VDT to use adjustable chairs and tables as well as non-glare screens, and to leave not less than five feet between the back of a VTD and the next workers. Resolution 409-90 contains the regulations that were approved on December 17, 1990. Though the regulations were not as demanding as the first draft, employers are expected within 30 months to bring most workstations into conformity with VDT safety standards.

Also, the city has set up a Video Display Terminal Advisory Committee to update health and safety information.

The New York and San Francisco ordinances show the mounting pressure on employers to address employees' concerns about the long term effects of the new office technology. As pointed out by Winn Rossch, "clusters of miscarriages have been associated with computer use, headaches and eye problems have been attributed to working at terminals, and even the dreaded word cancer has been whispered by researchers as a computer related health problem".

Since the personal computer itself is hardly ten years old, questions about the effects of long term use are impossible to answer definitively. AT&T and Pacific Bell claim that there is no reason for them to make changes before health effects are proven. A communication attorney for AT&T is reported to have said that "she is so confident there is no link between VDT exposure and health effects that she did not expect to pay workers' compensation claims, much less malicious conduct claims, in the future".

However, the responsibility of employers in work related injuries that involve the use of VDT and keyboards should be considered in light of recent court decisions. In February 1991, the Supreme Court let stand the convictions by a court in New York of two executives and their companies for endangering the health of employees. Given that the court took the same position in 1989 on a similar case from Illinois, managers should pay closer attention to the health issue.

The proliferation of writings in newspapers and the growing number of questions to talk show hosts on radio and television suggests that health risks from the use of new information technology is high on the public agenda. Indeed, there are growing concerns among office employees, union representatives, and legislators about the health risks of the new information technology. Paramount among them is the Carpal Tunnel Syndrome and Tenosynovitis -swelling or pain at the base of the hand because of prolonged use of a keyboard. The estimated cost of a single case of Carpal Tunnel Syndrome is said to be $25,000 to $40,000 in lost time, medical bills, and substitute employees.

The cost in the 90's will be much higher due to the general increase in the cost of medical expenses and the prospect of law suits against employers. According to the Bureau of Labour Statistics, repetitive strain injury (RSI) accounted for nearly half the workplace illnesses in private industry in 1988 as compared to only 18 percent in 1981. The Communications Workers Union contends that 30 to 60 percent of the respondents to a survey report repeated motion related disorders. The union blames fast work pace, large work volume, poorly designed workstations and failure to follow VDT safety rules.

Other reports point out to the growing number of law suits by journalists who are at risk because they spend long hours at the keyboard under deadline stress. A case in point is the $270 million lawsuit by journalists against Eastman Kodak Co., parent company of Atex Publishing Systems, maker of a popular news-room computer. Besides the health risks from repeated use of the keyboard, questions have been raised about the possible harmful effects of radiation from video display terminals. A recent report suggests that even the high frequency sounds a PC generates may cause headaches, tension, and stress. The report is based on several experiments by Caroline Dow and Douglas Covert and implies that women are more susceptible to the noise.

The term technostress describes the inability to cope with new computer technology in a healthy manner. Yet stress and lower productivity may also result when employees do not have a sense of control over their work. Electronic monitoring of key-strokes and programs that bring up the next document as soon as the work on the previous document is saved can lead to depression, anxiety, and withdrawal. A second reason for stress is that working with computers is highly sedentary and provide less opportunity to socialize.

Information technology is not limited to computers, and the stress it generates is not limited to coping with import, export, or manipulation of data. The beeper, cellular telephone, fax machine, and two-way tele-conferencing change the ways superiors and subordinates interact with each other. Coping with the change, if not the characteristics of these new ways, can be stressful. From an organizational point of view such non-computer devices can improve productivity. They allow subordinates to contact their supervisors or other key people in the organization, and it gives managers the option of getting in touch directly with subordinates that may have the answer to the problem they need to solve.

In either case, the organization may improve its response to unexpected situations. Yet, the organization that expects employees to wear beepers around the clock, use cellular telephones from their cars, keep fax machines at home or sit in front of a television camera for a live tele-conference may strain working relations and induce stress. The new information technology provides inducements for making home an extension of the office. It creates conditions that may lead to neglect of family time and responsibilities because of job related activities.

Isolated incidents of employees who refuse to carry a beeper after hours suggest that organizations may pay dearly for this convenience. Employees who experience deterioration of their health and family (or social) life may blame their employers even when there are other reasons for it. Thus, productivity gains by use of new information resources may be offset when the stress and health problems they induce take their toll on motivation and performance during regular working hours.

Questions about the safety, security, and health of employees because of the presence or use of information technology may require the development of a new job classification for information safety and security officers. The new breed of "guards," the information rangers, is not going to be armed with guns. They will possess advanced degrees and multi-disciplinary backgrounds. Their prior experience and training will allow them to identify the potential implications for their agencies from developments in areas such as engineering, physiology, economics, psychology, management, or law.

The duties of the information ranger will include safeguarding the integrity of the organization's information resources and the safety of its users. The information ranger will also be the key person for planning and coordinating emergency services for recovery of data in response to internal or external disruptions. According to a computer trade magazine, "in the face of lenient treatment for criminals who disrupt systems, companies are increasingly relying on individuals who can identify areas of risk and deal with them".

The magazine suggests that "these people have to formulate the plans, implement and test procedures to ensure that vital systems remain functioning or can be quickly restored to operation if disaster strikes". When it comes to information technology, security cannot be separated from safety. As pointed out earlier, increasing accessibility to the information, on and off the agency premises, increases the danger to the integrity of the system. The increased use of computer terminals may involve a health risk. The hazards involved in the use of video display terminals should not overshadow the possible risk to the physical safety of field employees.

The safety of individuals that use portable computers may be at stake when criminal elements desire to access government networks or to obtain data from the hard disks of the portable computers. Taken together, these possibilities suggest that safety and security are two sides of the same coin. To deal with all aspects of safety and security, the information ranger must have a high level of expertise in areas such as computer technology, criminology, occupational health, finance, and administration. They will have to be licensed, commissioned or certified so that they can conduct investigations and deal with other law enforcement agencies as warranted.

To retain their usefulness, information rangers will have to keep abreast of the constant changes in information technology, new threats to information integrity, protection of employees from health hazards, and client rights. The price tag for this continuing training is likely to be high but any attempt to reduce the frequency of such training may be counter productive. In July 1990, the Office of Management and Budget (OMB) announced its intent to place the burden of protecting federal data bases with agency heads.

Similar policies are likely to be established at the state and local levels of government. Given the high cost of retaining in-house computer safety and security experts will force public managers to make difficult choices. They may opt to play it safe and to incur the cost of reducing uncertainties and risks by paying the specialists up front. Or, they may take the chance that the disaster (that could have been prevented or reduced in scope by having a specialist on board) will not happen.

In the latter case managers are betting that the short term savings on security measures are real and will not lead to long term expenses and economic losses. In the first case, managers must gamble that the necessary resources for underwriting the cost of the new job classification and related expenses will not affect other activities of the agency and will not generate too much political turmoil. In the second case, the wager is that the savings (from postponing security and safety services) will exceed the liability for not having such services in house.

If agency heads choose to install Information Rangers, developing the support and mobilizing the resources for introducing this new job classification will entail a process similar to the one involving the introduction of the classification for Information Resources Manager (IRM). Eventually, public agencies will follow the trends that are already emerging in the private sector to coordinate and manage information resources at the highest level of the organization. The recent effort of the General Services Administration (GSA) to introduce a new job classification for what GSA names "Trail Bosses" indicates the trend to introduce new job classifications for dealing with the new reality of advanced information technology.

"Trail Boss" is the name GSA bestows on the senior managers it trains "to ride herd over the government's largest and most complex computer procurement" for their agencies. To participate in the program, an agency must develop a charter that lays out explicitly who is in charge and how the acquisition will be managed. Trail Bosses study everything from ethical questions to testifying before Congress, forecasting of information technology trends, handling contract legal issues, and dealing with vendors. Trail Bosses became necessary for dealing with the procurement process that became too complicated due to the high cost of new systems and litigation from vendors with high stakes in massive government contracts.

The complexity of information safety and security, the direct cost when a system is breached, and the prospect of indirect cost from litigation may resemble the issues involved in procurement. Thus the rationale for the new guards, the Information Rangers, may develop along the same lines of reasoning. Information Rangers may develop along the same lines of reasoning. Information Rangers, at the federal, state and local levels of government would have to form a network of their own. Such a network will be necessary for efficient and effective use of resources for the training, technical support, and mobilization of expert assistance in an emergency.

THE CHANGING SOCIAL CONTEXT OF WORK

The new information technology influences the welfare of the individual employee directly by influencing the health and safety aspects of work and indirectly by changing the social milieu of a job. By altering the social context of work the technology influences the nature of the relationships between the individual and the organization and thus, the behaviour of the organization.

With the proliferation of computer networks and telecommuting, managers are likely to see a change in group dynamics. To understand the change and to anticipate it, managers must understand the difference between a work group and a workgroup. A work group is a social entity with important social and psychological functions for the individual employee and for the organization. It can serve as a support group, or it can be a vehicle by which an employee can relate to the organization and to other groups. The work group establishes the norms of behaviour its members follow.

The group influences attitudes toward work, motivation and standards of excellence. A work group can evolve when co-workers report to a common supervisor, when they work together to complete a particular task, when their work situation (e.g., they work the night shift) differentiates them from other workers, or when they serve a particular clientele group. The work group develops when circumstances bring people together to facilitate interpersonal interactions and cooperation. A work group implies the existence of a lasting pattern of relationships.

Computer networks bring people together to create a workgroup out of what has (or has not) been a work group. The workgroup is very different from the work group. It is temporary, it fulfills a predefined technical purpose, and it does not, nor is it expected to fulfill any socio-psychological functions. A workgroup is a by-product of system engineering and the choices of hardware and software in use. The workgroup does not provide the employee with the kind of togetherness and the sense of belonging that results from membership in a work group. Under most circumstances employees wish to be accepted by members of their work group. Membership in such groups is not automatic. However, workers do not care, have a say, or make a choice about belonging to a workgroup.

A workgroup is an artificial entity. It exists only in a technical sense. Under the right circumstances, information technology can help an existing work group to mobilize its collective strength, helping members with marginal abilities to perform better. The workgroup harnesses the benefit of cooperation that does not depend on mutual interest and good will. Lindblom (1965) labeled this posture "adaptive adjustment" to denote a situation where a decision maker "simply adapts to decisions around him, that is make those decisions that he can make without first listing, as in negotiation, a response from other decision makers".

An organization may use computer networks and groupware, the software for mobilizing the contributions of several individuals, to disseminate a draft document for comments and suggestions. In doing so the organization may seek to mobilize the collective wisdom and insights of workgroup members as individuals rather than as members of the group. The result is an aggregate rather than a collective effort. The workgroup that is made up of all who worked on the document is not a work group because before, during, and after processing the document in question the involved individuals had no interpersonal relations. Each participant in the group was contributing to the document without considering the wishes, the identities or the needs of other participants.

Working on the same document does not help the creation of a group spirit and the workgroup is not dependent on it for survival. As soon as the task is over, the workgroup dissipates. For other tasks, new temporary workgroups will be formed. It is interesting to note that while group spirit is not a factor that influences the productivity of a workgroup the hardware and groupware in use can make a difference. In comparison, information technology cannot substitute for the group spirit of a work group. The quality of the technology is not likely to make a difference when the group's spirit is weak.

The introduction of the software and the hardware that make it possible to foster a workgroup is based on the recognition that most office work involves team work. Although the technical built-in features of most systems can facilitate cooperation and interaction among employees, information resources may not be conducive for initiating or developing team spirit. For reasons, like the ones listed below, information technology (except for some forms of computerized bulletin boards) can create the conditions for killing any chance for developing such spirit.

Information technology may work against creating a group spirit because, for one thing, it usually allows for multiple points of entry into the workgroup. As hardware and software become the gate keepers that allow or deny access to group resources, the natural boundaries of the group are defused. Intimacy, a sense of belonging, and the feeling of having some control over who is a member of the group and who is not, are missing when a workgroup is formed only by the sharing of information resources. Groups formed in this way are different from other groups at any work place. They lack common values and norms of behaviour that evolve from the interactions among members of the group.

Adhering to certain norms, in the case of workgroups, may be the result of using a particular configuration of software and hardware. Workgroup norms have to do with meeting technical needs of system users rather than social needs of group members. The norms are likely to be set for the workgroup by administrators in charge of common information resources. The evolution of workgroups becomes a function of the interactions between members of the workgroup and such administrators rather than the interactions among members of the workgroup.

As workgroups form, some work group managers may see changes in organizational behaviour productivity. To counteract some of the dysfunctional results of workgroups, it may be necessary to design organizations in a different way. Such designs should compensate for the fact that human touch and good interpersonal relations are important for dealing with contingencies. The existing information technology which fosters impersonal interactions with information resources and other members of the workgroup is incapable of dealing with situations that call for brain storming and use of fuzzy logic. Networking, for example, can facilitate the exchange of information but not necessarily the development of a preferred solution to a given problem.

Using the same database on a computer can make the interaction between any two members of a work group impersonal, indirect and without any relationship to the work of other users. In the past, dealing with the same client, using the same data base, having to attend the same meeting, or contributing to the creation of the same document required the involved employees to interact directly with each other. These interactions provided a basis for developing interpersonal relations and for forging a work group. True, the chemistry that results from interpersonal interactions can work the other way as well. Interpersonal relations that result from such interactions can enhance cooperation and smooth problems due to good will.

At other times, direct interactions among employees can lead to poor interpersonal relations. When this happens the involved employees may experience unnecessary obstacles and be forced to select inferior solutions to problems. With the new information technology, some interpersonal interactions become unnecessary. The common base for action is the use of the same data bank but the commonality of interest that results from interpersonal relations is gone. Users of a data base may not know the identity of other users. The handling and use of information are governed by the hardware and software that establish who can access, read, write, change, or copy which files.

The technology does not require one employee to consider the working needs of another who shares the same resource. The two may never interact directly, meet or discover each other's identity. The employees sharing a data base may be in different parts of the country, they may work for different agencies (or levels of government), or pursue unrelated goals. For example, a data bank of government payments may be used by one employee working for an agency that oversees contracted work while another user may be involved in the collection of overdue child support.

A work group must be small, relatively speaking, to allow a minimum level of direct and positive interactions among members of the group. Such an interaction is necessary for maintaining group identity. As the size of the work group increases, the direct interaction of any one member with most of the other members becomes less frequent. Group identity is lost. Those members of the group who continue to interact on a regular basis are likely to form a subgroup that may, or may not, keep in touch with the rest of the original group.

A workgroup, however, does not have to be of a certain size because it does not have to maintain an identity and a notion of affiliation among its members. A workgroup can be made up of an entire department or of a single subunit. It can be made up of a single work group or it can include members from many work groups from various agencies and across geographical locations. A workgroup emerges because hardware and software allow users to access a common data base and not because of any common goal or interest. The benefits from constant updating and maintenance of a single common data base (as a substitute for proprietary data banks for each user) may be sought by outside managers.

Such administrators may not use the data base themselves but may insist on creating one to improve productivity. In fact, not all members of the workgroup may consider as an advantage the need to use a common, rather than a proprietary, data bank. They may perceive some alleged benefits of a common repository of data as a cost. Members of the workgroup are likely to deal with the same clients (e.g., eligible contractors), report to the same oversight bodies (e.g., legislative bodies), or to be responsible for activities that can influence (or be influenced by) other events within the confines of a limited geographical location (e.g., local utilities).

IMPLICATIONS FOR HRM

The advances in information technology in general and in telecommunications in particular open new ways for accommodating employees with special needs. Such needs occur in employees with impairments to hearing, vision, speech, mobility, or the use of hands as well as those on maternity or extended sick leave. The new technology allows the workplace to be transplanted to the home so that the home-bound can remain meaningfully employed.

This flexibility by itself can make a difference in the mental health, self respect, recovery, and general functioning of the involved individuals. In particular, the ability to work from home by telecommuting may determine the economic feasibility of employment. In the past, the cost of special arrangements for transportation back and forth to the workplace, coupled with the cost of special provisions on site (e.g., for oxygen) forced many disabled individuals out of the work force.

It should be noted that often an employee may have to quit a job to care for a family member. In such cases the employee is hard hit economically on top of the psychological stress that results from the incapacity of a loved one. Telecommuting allows such employees to retain working habits and important skills that may help them to return to work one day. The continuing employment enables home-bound employees to retain important fringe benefits such as retirement, disability, and health insurance. The possible loss of valuable employees forced by circumstances to stay at home may be a source of future cost to society.

Last, but not least, continuing employment can help such individuals stay in touch with co-workers as an important support group. The loss of such support by itself can influence the ability of an employee to cope with a difficult situation at home. Following the enactment of the Americans with Disabilities Act of 1990, employers are required to take the necessary steps to accommodate the needs of employees with special needs. Issues of easy access to the workplace aside, information technology holds the key to successful implementation of this important public policy.

Special programs that translate speech to written words and vice versa allow employees that have difficulties speaking, hearing, seeing, or writing to function and to hold meaningful jobs that make use of their other skills and talents. Scanners, fax machines, speech synthesizers, optical imaging, and robotics removed some important constraints on the employment of individuals with special needs. More importantly, it allows such employees to function on the same level with other workers, to be subject to the same evaluation procedures, and to vie for the same careers. Accommodating individuals with functional impairment is not only the law; it is an economic necessity for dealing with the expected shrinking of the labour force as suggested by the 1988 Hudson's Institute Report Civil Service 2000.

It should be noted, however, that the architecture of modern information technology can undermine the ability of disabled employees to retain their jobs. The need to push more than one key at a time to operate a keyboard or a mouse or the need to read small print or graphic characters that cannot be translated easily to ASCII equivalents can spell the end of meaningful employment. Thus, as employers introduce new means for dealing with information to enhance productivity, they may push out the disabled. In particular, the trend toward graphic interface and object programming is perceived as a threat to the employment of people with vision impairments.

The issue seems not to be the cost of the technology for the disabled but the awareness of managers about that technology's existence. It seems that managers are not aware that there are inexpensive solutions to the technological problems the disabled may have in using information resources. The missing element is the education of managers about the availability of such devices and the new options for involving and accommodating the employee with special needs.

POSSIBLE FUNCTIONS AND DYSFUNCTIONS

Management of the organization's human resources must consider the implications of information technology on productivity, and the welfare of employees. While information technology can contribute to productivity, its potential for undermining it is just as potent. As organizations attempt to take advantage of its constructive features, managers must be aware of its limitations and the risks that result from using it. As Robert Solow, a Nobel laureate in economics put it "we see the computers everywhere but in the productivity statistics".

During the 1980s capital investment in hardware and software that averaged $9,000 per employee in the service industry resulted in productivity increase of a meager 0.2 per cent a year. This rate is much below the 5 per cent rate for the manufacturing sector that spends less than half as much on computer technology. Noonan reports that following the introduction of new office technology "the work week for the typical white-collar professional is 20per cent longer than it has been ten years ago. Yet during this same period, while-collar productivity declined"

The dysfunctional influence of information technology on the job content of middle managers deserves special attention. As organizations replace support staff with networks, groupware, E-mail systems, and cards that can send fax messages from within other programs, middle managers may spend only 27per cent of their time on typical management tasks and an increasing amount of time on activities that used to be the domain of secretaries and other support staff employees.

Reducing the number of subordinates to whom routine tasks cab be delegated amounts to subtle, even if unintended, demotion. Even when a middle manager does not realize it at first, reduction in staff can still influence moral and productivity. The reason is that while the new information technology forces managers to respond faster to developments within and outside the organization they can delegate less. The result is an imbalance among the four managerial functions: decision making/planning; organizing; staffing/actuating; and controlling.

As pressure on decision making/planning increases (because of the speedy dissemination of information), the ability of managers with fewer subordinates to adjust by the use of the organizing, staffing and controlling, shrinks. The paradox is that as information technology increases the pace of decision making, and thus the demands on the time of the executive, the administrator can relay less on support staff for assistance. As managers find that they must do all they did in the past plus some tasks they used to delegate (relegate?) to less experienced and lower-salaried employees, they are likely to experience growing stress and frustration.

A prudent approach for using the new information technology to enhance productivity requires managers to invest not only in the best hardware and software for the job but in expensive safeguards. Overlooking undesirable affects on employees' moral, safety, and security is as serious as underestimating possible threats to the integrity of operations and information systems. As information technology replaces employees, the art of improvisation as a management technique loses its value.

Managers may have the option of asking employees from other units to stay after hours or the option of hiring temporary help in improvising a solution to a problem. However, in the aftermath of a virus or any other information disaster, improvisations that involve simple infusion of labour cannot provide a solution. New information technology allows managers to retrieve and disseminate information about planned and ongoing activities. By using electronic mail (E-mail), fax, paging, and electronic bulletin boards (BBS), a manager can ascertain whether a particular employee or subunit is aware of critical information.

Networking and powerful software give managers instant access to all the data they need for status reports and the ability to spot emerging trends. This, in turn, makes it possible to anticipate problems and prepare for them. According to Paller (1990), the Postal Service, for example, relies on an executive information system (EIS) that uses colour graphs and charts to help managers pinpoint problems needing their attention. Raw data on agency performance is packaged into narrowly defined subject files on a mainframe. The information is updated monthly and a local area network (LAN) allows managers to access it. During the last two years, more than twenty five agencies have installed such systems.

To coordinate planning in anticipation of various contingencies and to adjust implementation to the parameters of specific situations, organizations will have to hire a new breed of experts, the Information Rangers. The Information Ranger can help the organization deal with issues of safety and security, but micro-management - i.e., fine tuning of operations, retention of loyalty and maintenance of the organizational culture - will still be part of the manager's job.

The new information technology can provide the manager with the means for dealing with some problems of micro-management. One example of the way the new technology can contribute to micro-management is the new capability of the unobtrusive monitoring of employee performance. By electronic retrieval, a manager may review the work completed by a subordinate and identify areas where additional training is needed. Indeed, there may be some questions about ethics and rights of privacy when undercover supervision is used. If the individual's rights can be safeguarded and issues of informed and prior consent can be settled, the ability of the manager to access work files without alarming the employee unnecessarily is not without merit.

Undercover supervision eliminates the anxiety and the threats that result from a request for a formal and open review of working files. Thus, unobtrusive supervision, by ethical managers and with the proper safeguards, can be less threatening to the employee's good feeling and self-esteem. As shown by the practices of companies such as IBM, Federal Express or Merick & Co., fair work-monitoring practices are possible. Such practices involve employees in developing fair monitoring practices and require managers to keep data confidential and to emphasize quality as well quotas.

Furthermore, dispatching an employee for a training session, because of an unobtrusive review, may not be perceived as punishment or an indication of a low performance rating. Such perception may influence motivation and reduce the willingness or ability of the employee to be trained. The use of Interactive Video Instruction (IVI) multi-media computer based training (CBT) programs, satellite hookups, and networking provides new opportunities to offer many kinds of in-house training, making training more feasible.

Managers are more likely to recommend such training when it does not involve the expenses of having to send the employee away to get the training. The ability to custom tailor the training to the special needs and time schedule of the employee and the agency increases the attractiveness of a remedial action. The marginal cost of providing remedial or advanced training simultaneously with other employees eliminates a possible stigma of being asked to participate in such training. Providing the training to other employees, for a reason other than as a corrective measure, increases the cost effectiveness of the training investment.

The same technology that allows the administrator to keep a low profile also offers ways to make the leadership of the organization more visible. With tele- and video-conferencing, desk-top publishing, electronic mail, the electronic bulletin boards, closed circuit television, satellite hookup, top officials can exchange information with more subordinates. For instance, they can invite first line employees to report directly to them on issues of great importance by way of a two-way tele-video-conference.

With the new technology, managers do not need to use middle management for disseminating or retrieving information. They can control and coordinate the activities of subunits directly through computer networks. Such top level managers can assert their leadership by providing all employees with an open and uncensored channel of communication (e.g., by using electronic mail or bulletin boards) to the executive suite.

Taking advantage of the new information resources to improve HRM does not relieve managers of their duty to contain the dysfunctional implications of new the technology. Reviewing the experience in the private sector, McConnell and Koch conclude that "what most companies do not realize is that this dysfunctional relationship between users and technology is not a technological problem. It is a problem of poor leadership at all levels of business and information systems management".

To compensate for the dysfunctional aspects of the new office technology, administrators must initiate new efforts to maintain the social infrastructure of the organization. Managers can turn a workgroup into a work group by providing employees with new opportunities to meet and to interact with each other. In order to realize savings on office space when employees work at home, organizations may have to pay their transportation to periodic retreats where they will be able to meet co-workers and relate to them as individuals.

In a similar way, liberal policies about the use of electronic bulletin boards can help organizations replace the informal communication system of yesteryear, making up for both its functional and dysfunctional attributes. It follows that the public sector should learn what was lost on the private sector during the seventies: in order to enjoy the benefits of productivity made possible by new technologies, managers should re-invest some of the savings in the organization.

2

International Technological Dualism

More than 30 years ago, Hans Singer (1970) introduced the concept of international technological dualism, by which he meant essentially unequal developments in the area of science and technology, between rich and poor countries. Here we suggest, first, that Singer's analysis remains highly relevant to our understanding of the technological relationships between these countries and we suggest, furthermore, that the prevailing approach to IT and development is a reflection of the same basic forces that give rise to past and present forms of international technological dualism.

Indeed, in certain key respects information technology may even strengthen such forces and thereby accentuate still further the problems described originally by Singer. First however, let us examine in some detail precisely what he meant by the concept. Thereafter, we re-appraise the main elements of the concept in the contemporary global context, including as it does, fundamental innovations in information and communication technology and attempts to apply such innovations in developing countries.

In essence, what Singer identified was a 'process of scientific and technological advance' that 'in all its stages - basic research, applied research and blueprinting - has been heavily concentrated in the richer countries'. Indeed, according to Singer (1970:62): 'The best estimate we can make at the present time is that measuring the distribution of advance by the distribution of inputs in the form of research and development expenditures, we find that 70 per cent of world expenditure is in the U.S., 25 per cent in Europe, and 2 per cent in the less developed countries.' The acute inequality of global R&D expenditures thus identified:

> Would not matter if the direction of advance, the scientific and technological priorities and the methods of solving scientific and technological problems, were independent of where the work is carried on. This, however, is patently not the case. The 98 per cent of research and development expenditures in the richer counties are spent on solving the problems which concern the richer countries, according to their own priorities, and on solving these problems by the methods and approaches appropriate to the factor endowment of the richer countries. In both respects - selection of problems and methods of solving them - the interests of the poorer countries would be bound to point in completely different directions. Yet the two-thirds of mankind with its different problems accounts for only 2 per cent of all expenditures - a discrepancy per capita ratio of no less than 100:1.

With respect to the divergent nature of technical change that would be dictated by the factor endowments prevailing in rich rather than poor countries. Point A represents a certain level of output on an arbitrarily chosen iso-cost line ED. Technical change in the figure is represented by reductions in the amounts of capital and labour that are required to produce the given level of output associated with point A. In the case of point R, for example, because less of both inputs are required to produce the same level of output as at A, the former combination dominates the latter in the sense that it is a more efficient technique at all factor price ratios. Conversely, A dominates all factor combinations within the area PAM, where more of both inputs are needed to produce the said level of output.

In Singer's analysis, the direction of technical change in actual practice is dictated by the concentration of R&D

expenditures in the developed countries, where, in general, labour is scarce relative to capital and innovations will consequently tend to take place in the area above AB and to the left of PA. Such innovations can be described as biased in the Hicksian sense that they lead to an increase in the ratio of capital to labour. (Note that biased technical change in this sense does not require that the absolute amount of both factors be reduced per unit of output.) Very few innovations, by contrast, would occur in the (capital-saving) area below AM and to the right of PC, given the paucity of R&D expenditures undertaken by the developing countries themselves, as noted earlier.

Even what little R&D does take place in the Third World, moreover, is not necessarily of the kind that would be dictated by the factor endowments and other conditions prevailing in those countries. For, as Singer further points out in his discussion of international technological dualism:

> The fact that the richer countries have such a virtual monopoly of research and development expenditures, as concretely expressed in terms of institutions, equipment, number of trained scientists and technologists, as well as virtual monopoly of deciding where the existing frontiers of knowledge are, has the further consequence that the activities of the small number of institutions and people, represented by the 2 per cent of research and development expenditures in the poorer countries, is also itself largely devoted to the problems and methods determined by the richer countries. Much of the present expenditures of the poorer countries represent a hopeless attempt to compete from an inferior position in solving the same kinds of problems by the same methods.

To some extent, this process, may, as Reddy suggests, take the passive form of 'a virtually unexamined and unquestioned introduction of alien and inappropriate guidelines, preferences and paradigms into the relevant institutions in the developing countries'. In part, however, the process described by Singer may also reflect a more active emulation of developed country scientists that international (and to large degree also national) rewards accrue to those working at the research frontiers.

Indeed, because these rewards are usually more easily won by working in the developed countries themselves, an international 'brain-drain' emerges, and constitutes the third dimension of Singer's concept of international technological dualism. As he himself put it, 'The existence of the richer countries, with their immensely superior facilities, and the glamour associated with work on their self-defined "frontiers of knowledge" exert a powerful attraction resulting in the well-known "brain drain"'. (In fact, even by the early 1970s the problem had assumed such importance those economists such as Bhagwati were proposing to tax professional migrants in order to raise revenue for the developing countries that suffered from the consequent loss of scarce human capital.)

For Singer then, the problem is not that the volume of accumulated knowledge has failed to increase over time. It has rather to do with the differential relevance of that body of knowledge to develop as opposed to developing nations. In particular, the latter have increasingly found them exposed to the types of technological advances that bear little or no relevance to their own particular problems and this in turn is due to international dualism, the fact that knowledge is accumulated by the richer countries, and in respect of the problems of the richer countries.

These are not the problems or methods of primary concern to the developing countries. The richer countries are mainly interested in sophisticated products, large markets, sophisticated production methods requiring large inputs of capital and high levels of skill and management while saving labour and raw materials. The poor countries by contrast are much more interested in simple products; simple designs, saving of capital and particularly land, reduction in skill requirements, and production for smaller markets. The potential impact of the increasing stock of knowledge - no doubt still very important and on balance useful to developing countries - has been largely offset by a tendency for each unit of this knowledge to become less and less useful to developing countries.

It is true that the technology thus emanating from the developed countries may still have some relevance for the more modern sectors of developing countries, but the resulting situation of growing internal technological dualism would then hardly be conducive to growth and development, as Singer himself recognized and others, such as Johnston and Kilby (1975) and Stewart (1977) have confirmed. As we see it, moreover, the main elements of international technological dualism thus described have continued to retain their general relevance in the contemporary world of IT and globalization. While noting the rapid rise of R&D expenditures in South Korea, Taiwan and Singapore over the past decades (and more modest increases in some other developing countries), Freeman and Hagedoorn (1995:37) for example, conclude that global R&D expenditures are nevertheless 'highly concentrated in the rich OECD countries'. While, at the other extreme, 'The Third World, on the most generous estimates, accounts for only about 6 per cent and without Chinprobably less than 4 per cent of global R&D'. If, therefore, the composition of global R&D has not changed markedly since the time when Singer originally discussed the problem, is there any indication that this type of investment has become more relevant to the problems of poor countries?

Perhaps the best answer to this question is provided in the 2001 version of the Human Development Report, which, after noting that 'research on and development of technologies for poor people's needs have long been under funded', goes on to suggest that 'Despite the possibilities of technological transformations, this continues to be the case'. Although there are few precise estimates of spending on developmental needs (itself 'a sign of the lack of attention paid to this problem'), the pharmaceutical industry is more revealing than most. More specifically, for example:

In 1992 less than 10 per cent of global spending on health research addressed 90 per cent of the global disease burden. Just 0.2 per cent, for example, was dedicated to research on pneumonia and diarrhoea - 11 per cent of the global disease burden. This funding gap creates research and medicine gaps. In 1995 more than 95,000 therapy-relevant scientific articles were published but only 182-0.2 per cent of the total - addressed tropical diseases. And of 1,223 new drugs marketed worldwide between 1975 and 1996, only 13 were developed to treat tropical diseases - and only 4 were the direct result of pharmaceutical industry research. Reallocating just 1 per cent of global spending on health research would provide an additional $700 million for priority research on poor people's maladies.

By the same reasoning, what one also needs to ask in the present context is whether the increased amounts of research spending in developing countries have become any more oriented to their own needs and problems than they seemed to be in the past (as discussed earlier). As in the case of developed country R&D, however, it is difficult and if not impossible to provide a specific answer to this question, given the same lack of empirical material.

Again as in the case of the developed countries, it is far from difficult to cite cases where R&D investments have generated innovations that are relevant to local low-income needs, such as small-scale tractors in India or low-cost computers in Brazil. Basing her view on a number of country case studies, Stewart, however, argues that such examples as these represent only a minority of cases within the innovations of the R&D institutions in developing countries there is tremendous potential for improving the productivity of traditional methods in Indian agriculture; this potential has not been realised partly because of deficient R&D. The study of technical change in Latin America indicated that no efforts had been made to channel innovations towards appropriate technology.

If this particular problem thus seems not to have been reduced to any significant degree over the past three decades or so, it is in all likelihood due to the same biases that link local R&D and other related institutions so strongly to the developed countries.

Only recently, for example, a prominent Brazilian scientist took critical note of how universities and research centres in developing countries 'have become isolated from the rest of the country in an ivory tower, more connected to research centres in Europe or the United States than to the obvious needs of industry, agriculture and education in their own countries. Heavy government bureaucracies wind up cultivating whatever science and technology is fashionable in the developed countries'.

Such an atmosphere, needless to say, only serves to increase the attraction of working in the developed countries themselves; an attraction that continues to erode the supply of crucial research and other capabilities in much of the Third World. Some of the most acute losses have occurred in small African, Caribbean and Central American countries, which according to one estimate, have lost no less than 30 per cent of individuals with a tertiary education. The same data source also records a substantial brain drain from Iran, Korea, the Philippines, and Taiwan Province of China. These figures tend to confirm that in several developing countries the outflow of highly educated individuals is still a major policy issue.

INFORMATION TECHNOLOGY AS INTERNATIONAL TECHNOLOGICAL DUALISM

Developed as it almost entirely was for the conditions prevailing in the developed countries (such as skilled labour, capital abundance, advanced infrastructure and high incomes), information technology applied in developing countries represents in many respects a reflection of the same pattern of international technological dualism that has helped to induce the pronounced and growing gap in incomes between rich and poor countries.

From this point of view that digital divide (defined as the unequal distribution of computers, Internet connections, fax machines and so on between countries) is merely another technological gap that emanates from and reflects the highly skewed distribution of global research expenditures between the North and the South. (Consider, e.g. the direction in which developed country research expenditures have transformed the characteristics of the once basic personal computer. Not only has this product become vastly more powerful and faster over time but (in the form, for instance of the Pentium 4 variety), it has also acquired a host of such high-income characteristics as DVD and CD-RW drives, a Trinitron monitor and highly sophisticated sound equipment.)

Relative to the period when the concept of international technological dualism was first introduced, however, the emergence of information and communication technologies has raised several new issues with regard to the internationalization of R&D and the possible implications thereof for scientific and technological forms of dualism between rich and poor countries. 'Prior to the mid-1970s', that is to say:

> One of the reasons stated by TNCs for not internationalising R&D was the difficulties involved with the supervision and control... But the introduction of new information and communication technologies (ICT) has significantly increased the scope for global sourcing of technologies. By the mid-1970s, the telecommunications, and computer industries were leaders in adopting the new methods of control for worldwide organization of R&D...
>
> In recent years, the R&D functions, especially in the high-tech industries such as... microelectronics...have become more science-based and research intensive... basic scientific knowledge is playing an increasingly crucial role in major technological advance; and many recent major innovations have occurred through cross-fertilization of different scientific disciplines. These ongoing paradigmatic changes in S&T are increasing the pressure on firms. These pressures can be met partly by increasing the in house R&D, both at home and abroad, or by the establishment with other firms of joint venture R&D or research cooperation with universities.

Since the 1980s, inter organizational technology cooperation has also become a widespread practice. If advances in communications technologies have thus made it feasible for multinational operations to internationalize (or globalize) their research operations, conditions in the labour market for R&D personnel are necessitating such operations. Indeed, one observer has gone so far as to argue that 'The key driving force for globalization of R&D in the 1990s has been the increasing demand for skilled scientists'. According to this view, an international market for science and technology personnel has arisen which extends beyond the OECD countries, to include 'uncommon countries...for international corporate R&D such as Israel, Brazil and India'.

As examples of this emerging trend, one can cite first the case of Texas Instruments in India, which performs geographically dispersed, but globally integrated R&D activities as a result of new information and communications technologies which allow the firm to 'send and receive the latest support information, design technology and applications information for its products and services'. In another example, Motorola has a paging device plant in Singapore employing 75 local engineers in its R&D centre. Indeed, according to the same source the 'Scriptor' pager was developed by local scientists at this centre, while yet another major American firm in the industry, Hewlett-Packard, uses its plant in Singapore as the 'global R&D and production centre for the company's portable ink-jet printers'.

From one point of view, this emerging propensity for R&D activities to spread themselves more widely across the developing world (or, at least a small part of it), clearly undermines the notion that developed countries undertake research activities only in the rich parts of the global economy. On the other hand, one also needs to consider the content of research expenditures thus dispersed to parts of the Third World. For, as noted earlier, one cannot necessarily assume that research expenditures undertaken in developing countries are directed solely to local needs and problems

Reddy's study of multinational firms in India, for example contains the most comprehensive information about the direction of R&D activities in that country and what is especially useful about his results is a comparison of 'new technologies' firms with firms in 'conventional' industries. In particular, whereas the latter conventionally perform some degree of adaptive R&D (i.e. adaptations of products and processes to the local environment), the former conduct considerably less of this type of R&D behaviour. Specifically, all the efforts to develop new products and processes for major world markets and to generate 'basic technology of a long term or exploratory nature for use by the corporate parent' took place in the new technologies firms, only 25 per cent of which undertake any adaptive type of R&D.

According to the same source, this suggests that in new technologies there is less need for product or process adaptation to the local market... Similarly, the development of products exclusively for the local market...by new technologies firms is also less, except in the case of biotechnology companies developing new plant varieties based on local soil and weather conditions. On the other hand, an overwhelming majority of new technologies firms are involved in developing products for the global markets, e.g., computers, communications, equipment, etc.

Thus, although globalization may be inducing some degree of dispersion of research activities outside the OECD area, the above evidence - limited as it is - suggests that the direction of the resulting innovations, such as 'global' products, may be even less relevant to the majority of those living in developing countries than the more adaptive type of research that was undertaken when subsidiaries were less closely integrated into global research and production networks. That research at least was intended to make products and technologies somewhat more relevant to developing country conditions (e.g. to the climate and environmental conditions).

At the same time, however, there is growing evidence from countries such as Brazil and India that local scientific personnel have developed innovations designed specifically for the income levels and other conditions prevailing in those countries. Both countries, for example have developed extremely low cost computers and Indian scientists have come up with a very low cost form of wireless local loop technology. And even in the developed countries themselves, there is a certain amount of research now being conducted on ways of bridging the digital divide by means of low cost information technologies (such as some of the research programmes at the Media Lab of the Massachusetts Institute of Technology).

Changes in the worldwide organization of R&D are not just confined to intra-firm locational behaviour (as just described) but also include various types of cooperative ventures between independent firms. It has been further suggested that these new coordination mechanisms, such as strategic alliances, may grant developing countries an opportunity to share in the generation of innovations in IT.

Here too however, there is doubt whether any such arrangements entered into by developing country firms are likely to address poor country concerns and needs in the area of information and communications technologies. For while there are numerous developing countries that participated in such alliances between 1984-1994, and while such participation may have enabled the firms concerned to gain access to knowledge that would otherwise have been inaccessible, there are again serious doubts as to whether the resulting innovations have had much, if anything, to do with the problems of poor people (though again there is very little evidence to make an assessment one way or the other).

TECHNOLOGICAL SYSTEMS

To an even greater extent than is true of most other technologies, IT, especially in its more sophisticated forms such as the Internet, is reliant on a wide variety of complementary inputs, which collectively, one can usefully describe as a technological system, following Stewart and James and Khan. The former, for example, has argued that at any point of time, techniques tend to be developed against a background of a particular technology package. ...

Any single technical innovation has to fit in with the rest of the system both in terms of the requirements it imposes for inputs, and in terms of the demand for the goods. A new technique must use inputs that are available or can be made available, and must provide output which will fit into production if it is an intermediate good; or into consumption patterns if it is a consumer good...There are technological linkages between different parts of the system which mean that much of technology comes as a package, which cannot be separated and introduced bit-by-bit, but which goes together.

In the specific case of the Internet, for example, the accompanying inputs that form part of the technology system in most developed countries are simply not available in the remote, rural areas of the Third World. Providing such inputs adds thus greatly to the costs of Internet provision. Kenny (2002:9-10), for example, has shown that the cost of telephony alone, will make Internet access unaffordable for the poorest groups in rural areas of developing countries. To this already substantial cost, one needs to add the additional average costs of Internet access, including as they do the need to supply the missing elements of the technology system in which this innovation belongs. In particular,

A recent estimate for the cost of Internet access in Mozambique... suggests that the annualised fixed costs of access to one Internet enabled computer (excluding telephone installation and rental but including equipment costs plus yearly Internet fee for unlimited use) were $1,172 per year. Services for a part-time technician to support users are likely to add at least another $2,000. On top of these costs are those for electricity, call charges and housing, which can be very significant in rural areas.

Shakeel et al (2001) estimate off-grid power costs per Internet enabled computer at about $4,000 fixed and $200 recurrent costs, for example. Providing Internet access is made more complex if [as seems often to be the case] there are no roads on which to travel to repair broken equipment, or if technicians have to travel long distances to assist remote facilities - again this is frequently the case in poor, rural areas.

Faced with such daunting cost estimates as these the donor community recognized that universal service (providing individual households with the new technologies) needed to be replaced by universal access (i.e. providing poor rural communities with communal services) and this in turn took the form mainly of so-called telecentres.

THE DONOR RESPONSE: UNIVERSAL ACCESS VIA TELECENTRES

Telecentres, write Oestmann and Dymond (2001:1) 'have been hailed as the solution to development problems around the world because of their ability to provide desperately needed access to information and communication technologies'. The same authors provide a useful summary of both the concept and the history of such widely touted institutions. As they (p. 3) put it:

Telecentres may be defined as strategically located facilities providing public access to ICT-based services and applications. They are typically equipped with some combination of:

- Telecommunication services such as telephony, fax, e-mail and Internet (via dial-up or ISDN, high-speed telecommunications network);
- Office equipment such as computers, CD-ROM, printers and photocopiers;
- Multimedia hardware and software, including radio, TV and video; and
- Meeting spaces for local business or community use, training and so on.

While facilities and usage vary across telecentres, all reflect the intention to address the issues of access by providing technology, develop human capacity and encourage social and economic development. Depending on the size and extent of the services provided, these centres are usually operated by a manager and a small number of staff who may be part-timers or volunteers. Originating in Sweden around 1985, telecentres (also known as 'telecottages') experienced fairly rapid growth in Western Europe and other industrialised countries where rural isolation, lack of purchasing power & low-quality telecommunications and information technology facilities were seen to be a hindrance to participation in the information economy.

By 1994, there were more than 230 tele-centres in Australia, Austria, Canada, Denmark, Finland, Germany, Ireland, Japan, Norway, Sweden, the UK and the USA. The idea then spread and has become adapted to the needs of emerging markets and developing countries. Hungary is the first country in Central Europe to establish a large number of rural telecottages (more than 150). It is difficult to assess with any degree of precision how far telecentres have spread in developing countries. Such evidence as is available, however, indicates that the degree of diffusion is already far from negligible.

Oestmann and Dymond (2001), for example, suggest that Telecentre Projects can be found in at least 21 developing countries, while many more such endeavours are still in the planning or pilot stage. Within some of these countries, moreover, the numbers of telecentres may already run well into the hundreds. South Africa, for example, is reported by one source to have as many as 500 multi-purpose community telecentres (UNESCO 2003).

As far as rates of telecentre growth are concerned, Fuchs (2000:1) has suggested that, with the help, often, of international aid donors at least several hundred are being established per annum in developing countries. Donor interest in Telecentre Projects, one should note, is concentrated on 'the creation of multi-purpose telecentres - providing computers, e-mail and Internet, not just telephones and fax - which are expensive to install, operate and maintain'.

This predisposition, we suggest, is far from peculiar to IT. Indeed, it has long been recognized that donors investing in developing countries tend to favour large-scale, capital- and foreign exchange-intensive projects. The explanation, now as then, has to do with the internal procedures and incentives in the donor institutions themselves. Although she was by no means the first to identify the forces in question, Stewart has described them with an unusual degree of clarify. To begin with:

An overwhelming objective of aid administration in many cases is to meet their target flow of finance, while ensuring that the projects financed meet the procedures that have been laid down. Questions of project efficiency and social desirability often come second. It is always easier to meet financial flow targets with a few big projects than with a multitude of small ones. Moreover, many small project managers may not be able to fulfil the mandatory auditing requirements.

When these objectives are combined with tied aid (as frequently is the case with bilateral donors), the above-mentioned propensity towards large-scale, capital-intensive and highly costly types of telecentres becomes virtually inevitable. On the other hand, 'Multilateral aid donors normally finance only the foreign exchange component of the capital cost of a project which automatically imparts a bias in favour of projects with heavy capital costs and a high foreign exchange component of the capital costs'.

EVALUATING TELECENTRES

Most of those who have studied the performance of large-scale, donor-funded telecentres in developing countries tend to arrive at the same basic conclusion, namely, that with few exceptions and on most indices of performance, these projects have performed rather poorly. The UNDP, for example, is an international institution that is generally sympathetic to the use of IT in developing countries. However, the same institution (UNDP 2001:23) points out that:

> The evaluative evidence of numerous donor-funded telecentre efforts - including several high profile initiatives in Africa - reveal fundamental problems and limitations. For example, three wide-ranging assessments of the telecentre experience in Africa, Latin America and the Indian sub-continent reveal that none of the major donor-funded initiatives have managed to become self-sustaining, and most have not achieved their expected development outcomes.

Similar conclusions have also been reached by Oestmann and Dymond (2001:5) who conducted a review of telecentres for the Commonwealth of Learning. After noting that 'telecentres are praised as a crucial development tool and have considerable potential', these authors go on to indicate that 'the data available on rural demand and usage of the Internet in such centres suggest that this is not sufficiently realised. A survey of telecentres in South Africa found that personal computers and the Internet were severely underutilised...It would also appear that computer training has increased Internet and personal computer usage in South African telecentres only minimally'.

In perhaps the most extensive review of community telecentres yet undertaken, however, the Canadian International Development Resource Centre (IBRD) conducted a sample study of telecentres in Uganda, Mali, Mozambique, South Africa and Senegal. Though the results of the survey will be officially presented at a conference hosted by the Acacia Initiative of the IDRC in April 2003, the basic findings are already available. (Note that the telecentres in all five countries offered similar services, including Internet access.)

Before presenting the most salient of those results in the present context, note that the summary of the book produced by the IDRC includes the statement that 'Although still surrounded by many unknowns, it is believed that as a delivery model for ICTs, telecentres have the potential to transform the lives and livelihoods of many in the developing world and even those in remote locations in developing countries.'

Yet, at the same time, that potential scarcely seems to have been realized. For, in spite of the fact that the telecentres in the five countries noted earlier have brought many people into contact with IT, it remains true that still a small percentage of the total population was using the telecentre facilities. Users are shown to have been disadvantaged on the basis of age, gender, education, literacy levels, and socioeconomic status. A striking observation is the absence of old people at the telecentres. Education appeared to be a key determinant of telecentre use. A popular view expressed by respondents was that telecentre services were for the elite or educated...low or non-use for some services was reported, for the Internet and email in the more rural MCTs in Uganda, Mozambique and Mali.

Finally, as argued by Kenny (2002:1), the experience with telecentres can usefully be viewed in terms of the social costs and benefits to which they give rise. In particular, the same author convincingly shows that, in spite of the growing popularity of Internet-based telecentres, these institutions tend to produce a very low ratio of benefits to costs in the context of poor, rural communities in the Third World. Thus, in spite of the 'movement in the development community pushing for the widespread rollout of community access points to the Internet as a tool for direct poverty relief', the problem, as Kenny sees it, is that:

The nature of extreme poverty in LDCs - very low incomes, subsistence and unskilled wage labour as the dominant income source, food as the dominant consumption good, low education and high illiteracy, minority language group status and rural location - points to an unsustainably high cost and relatively low benefit of direct Internet service provision through telecentres to the very poor. This might suggest that the push for Universal Internet access as a tool for poverty relief is misplaced.

Though he does not cast his argument in terms of international technological dualism or the diverse nature of technological systems, Kenny's list of problems associated with Internet-based telecentres in poor, rural areas has in fact much to do with these particular concepts. Recall from that earlier discussion - especially the parts dealing with the international technological system - the suggestion that technologies developed in and for developed countries tend to have little or no relevance to the poorest deciles of those living as they do, largely in the rural areas of developing countries. Now consider that supposition in relation to a description of telecentres in developing countries, which runs as follows:

There are some economies in which telecentres might be rational. They are those with good access to reticulated electricity, existing telecommunications networks, high population densities, and cash economies. In other words, telecentres are the product of, and designed for, cities very like the ones inhabited by the people who came up with the ideas for telecentres in the first place. However, since the world in which telecentres are supposed to deliver their benefits is very often a small town or rural community with poor infrastructure and minimal cash economy, there are fundamental gaps between the requirements of the telecentre model and their environment.

The same author goes on to point out, what in our terms, are the many problems associated with the insertion of modern technological systems into systems that are more reflective of traditional (often precapitalist) modes of economic behaviour. And while our earlier discussion of this concept was cast in rather general terms, the citation here refers specifically to IT and more specifically still, to the recent Pentium or equivalent [which] is the product of an economy from which serious dust and water intrusion, physical assaults, and major power fluctuations are excluded as a matter of course. The only way the Pentium [and by extension the Internet] can function in an LDC is to import a slice of its native economy with it. That requires sealable windows and doors, air conditioning, and large wedges of money.

Mardle alludes also to the need for electricity, satellite Internet and so forth. 'Then', once these are supplied, 'we [in the West] hand this over-capitalized, souped-up, expensive system over to the local community', whose task becomes one of making the project 'economically viable'.

The point that is being raised here is in fact a crucial one for the viability of Internet-based telecentres in developing countries. The point being that these imported structures form part of an extensive socioeconomic system (or package), which needs to be supplied to the recipient country in the Third World, if the technological part of the package is to function at all. And even if many such components can indeed be supplied by aid-donors (at a formidable cost), there are other parts of the package that cannot be so supplied (at least in the short to medium run).

Consider, for example, illiteracy and cultural attitudes to IT, which in the African case mentioned earlier, seemed to be crucial barriers to Internet access. Or again, take the bias against women users, which in that same case, was also clearly documented. Not least, moreover, is the fact that even literate users of the Internet will be very hard put to find relevant material in his or her particular local language (with English being by far the most common language used on the Internet). The essential point about these problems is not that they cannot be solved. It is rather that this will take quite some time: time which a newly established telecentre simply cannot afford if it is to reach the poor people that it purports to help.

The concept of Internet-based telecentres originated in and for the circumstances prevailing in the developed countries. As with much else in the technological relationships between rich and poor countries, this model has been incorporated by many segments of the international development community into their current thinking. Indeed, there are many elements of this community that view Internet-based telecentres as a crucial vehicle for assisting the vast numbers of poor rural communities in the Third World. And largely as a result of this prevailing view (or in its most elaborate form a paradigm for IT and development), so-called multi-purpose community telecentres have seen rapid growth in many areas of the developing world.

Our review of the admittedly rather scant evidence of the Telecentre experience, suggests, however, that it has provided minimal support to the poor, rural communities in the developing countries. In particular, the vast majority of that group has barely even come into contact with the Internet service thus provided (mostly by international aid-donors). More generally, following Kenny (2002), one can say with some degree of empirical backing that the social benefits of Internet-based Telecentre projects have been very low in relation to the high costs that they clearly entail.

Though there are many and varied reasons for this generally disappointing outcome, we have argued that the basic problem can be traced back to the neglect, in theory and practice, of several key concepts that were advanced in the technology and development literature as early as 1970. Briefly summarized, those concepts warn against the import of technologies from developed countries, partly because those technologies tend to be irrelevant to the needs of the impoverished rural communities in developing countries.

At the same time, however, because technologies form part of a much wider socio-economic system, in order for the Internet-based telecentres (or any foreign technology for that matter) to function, the entire system needs to be replicated in the places where they are located. The problem is then that while some elements of the technological package can be imported (albeit at prohibitively high costs), others simply cannot be (at least in the short to medium run). I am referring here, for example, to illiteracy, cultural attitudes to new technology, and engaging villagers in the Telecentre project.

3

The Information Economy

This chapter considers the nature of the IT industry today, including the role of producers of hardware (computing and telecommunications) and software, publishers of information, retailers and consultants. This discussion is illustrated by a number of case studies of different IT firms, mostly in the words of the organizations themselves. The chapter introduces the importance of two kinds of complex global networks. The first is the physical network of electronic communications which links computer systems across the world and enables multi-media connections between people and organizations of all sorts. The growth of this network is considered here; the social and political implications of this development are considered further in later chapters.

The second is an economic network or global marketplace. The global IT industry has contributed to the first and is a part of the second. We consider the role of multinational industries and the interdependence between information technologies in more detail.

Finally, this chapter considers the importance of information technology in contemporary society as a whole - examining the idea that information and its technology is the dominating characteristic of the age. We examine in more detail the nature of the 'information economy' and its implications for levels of employment.

IT FIRMS

It can be seen that the modern information and communication industry is a perhaps uniquely complex one. A preliminary distinction may be drawn between the producers of different types of communication goods and services, but in practice there is an increasing trend towards the integration of firms across categories. Each of these categories will be considered in turn, before the issues raised by the structural changes occurring at lightning pace within the industry are looked at.

The role of hardware suppliers seems, on the face of it, a straightforward one which has, seemingly, much in common with old-fashioned nineteenth-century industrial manufacturing operations. Raw materials may be presumed to come in the gates at one end of the works to emerge from the production line some time later as goods to be sold to consumers, the price of the goods reflecting the high cost of the sophisticated labour, machinery and materials employed. These assumptions are, however, largely false.

So called original equipment manufacturers (OEMs) of, say, personal computers are largely assemblers of components such as silicon chips, hard drives, equipment cases, cathode ray tubes, etc. The components will commonly have come from numerous countries and several continents. Some components will be from other manufacturers who may be thought of as being within the industry; others may come from general engineering or plastic moulding suppliers, for example. The value of the product often has little relation to the cost of materials, labour or even what may be colossally expensive machinery. Instead the value of the product will frequently depend upon the originality of its design and its usefulness to the buyer, who may well be another manufacturer or a supplier of information services.

It is worth highlighting that the technology - and hence the manufacturing techniques - employed is constantly changing so that, for instance, the manufacturing of televisions, telephones, and computers, which once were clearly separate products, is now clearly an overlapping set of processes sharing components, suppliers and customers. The category of software suppliers is obviously a much newer one than that of hardware manufacturer. It too can be easily misinterpreted.

It may evoke the image of a small group of millionaire teenage 'geeks' overdosing on Coca-Cola in an air-conditioned 'campus' in Silicon Valley, California, producing computer games for PC fanatics across the world. Such operations do exist, but most software houses differ from this in several respects. For instance, many software houses are now in India, which has produced few e-commerce millionaires. Many software operations are now tied commercially to hardware manufacturers - e.g. games producers may be tied to console manufacturers, or operating system developers to specific OEMs.

Other software operations may be serving the needs of a specific industry and have close links to them. Thus an aircraft manufacturer may take over a supplier of aircraft simulation software. Many software suppliers are engaged in the development of 'bespoke' software for specific firms to meet specific needs. For example the British firm, Sage, specializes in the production of accounting software.

AN ORIGINAL EQUIPMENT MANUFACTURER: DELL

Dell, founded in 1984 by Michael Dell, with its headquarters in Austin, Texas, became the world's largest seller of PCs in the third quarter of 2001. It had a turnover of $31.8 billion in 2000/1. It employs 34,000 'team-members' worldwide. Although best known for PC manufacture,

Dell is a major producer of powerful servers, and also offers consulting and on-line services and sells third-party software and peripherals. Dell pioneered a direct sales strategy for selling computers, being the first company to record $1 million per day in on-line sales (in 1997), and now conducts the majority of its sales through its website. The site handles 650 million page requests per quarter in 21 languages and 40 currencies. Customers can obtain information about the progress of their own orders, and suppliers can share detailed information about Dell's product quality and inventory on-line through a secure site.

Dell prides itself on minimizing its inventory by the use of Just-in-Time manufacturing to order. In 2000 it cut its average inventory (stock) holdings from six days' supply in the previous year to four. Production is concentrated in six regional plants (including two in the USA and one in China), with the one in Limerick, Republic of Ireland, serving Europe, the Middle East and Africa. The company has proved financially extremely successful, with one share bought on 22 June 1988 for $8.50, when stock was first offered publicly, being worth $2,392 at 2 November 2001.

A SOFTWARE HOUSE: BORLAND INTERNATIONAL

Borland is a leading provider of high performance e-business implementation solutions. Borland is the vendor of choice for professional e-business solution providers who demand a vendor-independent implementation platform that supports rapid time to market, high productivity, performance and availability.

Founded in 1983, Borland is headquartered in Scotts Valley, California, with operations worldwide. Borland provides customers with e-business implementation platforms designed to increase developer productivity and reduce time to market for enterprise software projects. These platforms consist of software products that help businesses to excel in all phases of the implementation process: development, deployment, and management of e-business applications.

For development, we offer JBuilder, C+ Builder, Delphi, and Kylix. Our deployment products include InterBase, Borland AppServer, and VisiBroker. To manage these systems, we offer AppCenter, a visual distributed application management solution.

Borland is committed to all major computing platforms as well as to the open standards of the Internet. Further, through the online developer community and an e-commerce site, community.borland.com, we provide service and support for software developers around the world. This resource site supports the developer community with a range of technical information, value-added services, and third-party products.

In addition to our products, we offer a wide range of consulting, training and support services to customers. The process of developing new high technology products and solutions is inherently complex and uncertain. It requires, among other things, innovation and accurate anticipation of customers' changing needs and emerging technological trends. Without the introduction of new products, services and enhancements, our products and services can rapidly become technologically obsolete, in which case revenues could be materially and adversely affected. Furthermore, there can be no assurance that such new products and services, if and when introduced, will achieve market acceptance.

We are recognized for providing high-quality, innovative software tools for customers seeking greater productivity and performance. We believe that our ability to develop innovative and successful products depends in large part upon successfully executing product planning strategies, research and development activities and our ability to attract, hire and retain highly qualified engineers and product management personnel. We plan to continue to invest in the area of research and development in the coming year. Research and development expenses for the year ended December 31, 2000, were $42.5 million.

In November 2000, we completed the acquisition of Bedouin, Inc., a Chicago-based software company. The acquisition is expected to accelerate our entry into the market for hosted development services (HDS). Borland intends to deliver a platform for developers to build, deploy and manage applications via the Internet. As presently contemplated, hosted development services would be available on the Internet to developers at the individual, project and enterprise levels.

A primary focus during the year ending December 31, 2001 is the growth of our direct sales organization. In the year ended December 31, 2000, more than a quarter of our revenue was derived from this direct sales organization. In addition, we market and distribute products worldwide through our own e-commerce Internet site, independent distributors, dealers, value-added resellers and independent software vendors.

We sell our products to a broad customer base, which includes businesses, educational institutions, government bodies and individual software developers. As we generally ship products upon receipt of orders, backlog is neither significant nor should it be detrimental to our future revenues.

We conduct operations and sell products outside the U.S. and maintain overseas offices in Australia, Brazil, Canada, France, Germany, Hong Kong, Japan, Netherlands, Singapore, Taiwan, Sweden and the United Kingdom, and, as part of our continuing global expansion, are in the process of opening offices in the People's Republic of China, South Korea and India. In addition to our research and development facilities in Scotts Valley, California, San Mateo, California and Chicago, Illinois, we also maintain research and development facilities in Australia, Japan and Singapore.

International net revenues (excluding exports from the U.S.) accounted for approximately 55 per cent of our net revenues in our fiscal year ending December 31, 2000. We contract with third parties for replication of CD-ROM discs, printing and production of packaging materials and assembly of final product packages for shipment to customers. Our products are principally sold in CD-ROM form together with user manuals. Some of our products are delivered directly by Borland via electronic download from the Internet.

The computer software industry is an intensely competitive industry. Rapid change, new and emerging technologies and fierce competition characterize the industry.

The pace of change has accelerated due to the emergence of the Internet and corporate Intranets and new programming languages. We face intense competition in the development and marketing of our software products and services.

To the extent that we are unable to obtain information regarding existing and future operating systems from the developers of (operating) systems, the release of our products for such systems may be delayed or may not be competitive. For example, Microsoft Corporation, a significant competitor to our Delphi and C++ Builder products, is the developer of the Windows operating environments. Microsoft Corporation has announced that it intends to include increased middleware functionality in future versions of its Windows 2000 operating system.

Microsoft Corporation has also introduced a product that includes certain basic application server functionality. The bundling of competing functionality in versions of Windows products requires us to compete with Microsoft Corporation in the Windows marketplace where Microsoft Corporation has certain inherent advantages due to its substantially greater financial, technical, marketing and other resources, greater name recognition, a larger installed base and the integration of its middleware functionality with Windows.

We rely on a combination of patent, copyright, trademark, trade secret laws, non-disclosure agreements and other intellectual property protection methods to protect our intellectual property. Despite our efforts to protect our intellectual property rights, it may be possible for an unauthorized third party to copy certain portions of our products or to reverse-engineer or obtain and use technology or other information that we regard as proprietary. In addition, the laws of certain foreign countries do not protect rights in intellectual property to the same extent as do the laws of the United States.

As of March 2, 2001, we employed approximately 934 employees, approximately 483 in the United States and 451 overseas. None of our U.S. employees are represented by a labour union.

The most obvious and long-established infrastructure operators are the public telecommunications operators (PTOs). In most of Europe, until recently, this meant a publicly owned subsidiary of the Post Office, with a monopoly over the supply of telephone lines. Government policies of privatization, and the development of alternative telephone technologies such as broadband cable systems and mobile phones using broadcasting, have generated much competition in recent years. In the USA the Bell telephone system was broken up in an anti-monopoly action much earlier, whilst many Third World countries retain public monopoly systems. Other infrastructure operators include conventional broadcasting organizations, suppliers of out-sourced organizational networks and the operators of communication satellites.

The term 'publisher' may suggest a faded gentleman with inky fingers proudly clutching a dusty hardback novel. It does still encompass the producers of enormous quantities of print materials - including newspapers, magazines, trade catalogues and advertising flyers. The new IT has made possible the production of more paper rather than replaced it! All printers now make intensive use of information technology to prepare and produce their materials. In this context publishing also includes all those who use IT to produce communications commercially. This would include broadcasters on radio and television, film studios, the sellers and distributors of videos, CD-ROMs of all descriptions, and the designers and operators of websites.

Each of these activities is a complicated commercial operation and is frequently carried out by a series of separate enterprises. Most academic books, for instance, are still written on a freelance (self-employed) basis by authors who draw upon the information resources of a university. Proof correction, and the supply of illustrations, may well also be carried out by other contractors to the publisher. Most publishers contract out the printing and binding of books to independent firms. Many also employ public relations, advertising, legal and accounting firms. Virtually all sell through wholesalers, bookshops and via the web. Other activities such as film production, or TV broadcasting, may well employ many more firms working together through contracts.

However, it is clear that there are many advantages to be gained by publishing across several media simultaneously. A good example being where a novel can be serialized in newspapers or magazines, translated for foreign markets, adapted for television, film and video, and even turned into an interactive computer game - not to mention being the basis for T-shirts and toys. Consequently many media firms have amalgamated into large, often multinational, cross-media groups which can cooperate in translating one product idea into numerous media.

AN INFRASTRUCTURE OPERATOR: AT&T CORP

The AT&T Corp. is the US equivalent of British Telecom. Formerly known as the American Telephone and Telegraph Company, it is a leading provider of global communications services, and the largest telecommunications company in the United States. Its main services include AT&T Wireless, AT&T WorldNet®, AT&T Solutions consulting, the AT&T Universal Card and the long-distance services.

Up to 1984, AT&T was the parent company of the Bell System, the privately owned, but government regulated, enterprise that formerly provided most telecommunications services in the United States. From then until 1996, AT&T was an integrated provider of communications services and products, network equipment and computer systems.

AT&T was originally founded in New York as a wholly owned subsidiary of the American Bell Telephone Company in 1885. At first, it managed and expanded the long-distance business of American Bell and its licensees. It remained the 'long-distance company' until 1899 when, in a corporate reorganization, it took over the business and property of American Bell and became the parent company of the Bell System.

AT&T has often been a pioneer: in 1927 the company began the first commercial transatlantic telephone service to

London using two-way radio. In 1950, AT&T opened its first microwave relay system between New York and Chicago, and subsequently added considerable microwave capacity to its nationwide long-distance network. In 1956, the first transatlantic submarine telephone cable, TAT-1, service to Europe began. In 1962, AT&T placed Telstar I, the first commercial communications satellite, in orbit.

AT&T and the Bell System were, in effect, a legally sanctioned but regulated monopoly. AT&T president Theodore Vail argued as early as 1907 that telephone technology would operate most efficiently as a monopoly providing universal service. Government regulation, 'provided it is independent, intelligent, considerate, thorough and just', could be a reasonable substitute for the workings of competition.

In 1949, an 'anti-trust' suit was filed which led in 1956 to a 'consent decree' agreed by AT&T and the Department of Justice, by which the company agreed to limit its activities to the regulated business of the national telephone system and government work. Another anti-trust suit by the US government began in 1974 and led to the January 1982 settlement in which AT&T agreed to divest itself of the wholly owned Bell operating companies that provided local exchange service. The US Department of Justice agreed to lift the constraints of the 1956 decree in return. Divestiture took place on January 1, 1984, and the new AT&T and seven regional telephone holding companies replaced the Bell system.

On January 1, 1984 AT&T started as a new company with only $34 billion of its former $149.5 billion in assets. Only 373,000 of its former 1,009,000 employees remained. Even the famous Bell logo and name was lost to the regional telephone companies - excepting for the name's use in Bell Labs. The new logo was a stylized globe accompanied by the monogram 'AT&T'.

This was seen by the company as releasing it from its former legal shackles, and from the increasing difficulty of working in old ways in a new information age. The technology developed at AT&T Bell Laboratories could now be used freely to compete in world markets.

Success in the new environment required a drastic change in corporate culture. The Bell System's culture stressed service, technological innovation, excellence, and reliability, and within a non-competitive framework of taking however much time and money it took to get things done right. The new company had to become a much more customer-focused organization. A task which proved far more complex and difficult than anyone imagined at the time.

Optimists within AT&T point out that the competition of over 400 rivals has greatly reduced the cost of telecommunications products and services by 60 per cent since 1984 whilst improving quality overall. AT&T's revenues have continued to grow and its financial resources have remained strong despite a rapidly changing environment. This has helped finance continued growth and improvement, including a multi-billion-dollar digitalization of the entire network, a continued move into the international market and major acquisitions and mergers. Mergers with major computing and cellular telephone companies (NCR and McCaw Cellullar) in the early 1990s helped the company acquire expertise and resources in these areas.

However, in 1995 AT&T announced a split into three more specialized companies: today's AT&T, which specializes in communication services; Lucent Technologies, a systems and technology company, which provides communications products rather than services; and NCR Corp., which is mainly a computer business. Lucent and NCR were hived off during 1996.

A 'PUBLISHER': ALTAVISTA

The AltaVista Company in its own words:

AltaVista is the Internet's premier search network that integrates unique technology and services to deliver relevant results faster for both individuals and Web-based businesses. The AltaVista Network enables you to unlock the unlimited potential of the Internet, by providing you with the most relevant and immediate results from a wealth of Internet resources.

Since our inception in 1995, AltaVista has taken a deliberate course of action to provide Web enthusiasts with a broad range of Internet search services and, through our proven technology, has succeeded in delivering relevant and useful information faster. Today, AltaVista delivers the ultimate Internet experience through the utilisation of cutting edge technology, numerous international and regional Web indexes as well as a multitude of search related features all designed to give users the best possible search experience on the Internet.

AltaVista's search technology has consistently been a performance leader since it was pioneered by the company as one of the first search services ever available, measured both by users and objective outside sources. AltaVista continues to revolutionise how users and partners find the most relevant content, information, products, and services available through the Internet.

AltaVista is committed to delivering best-of-breed Web results to our key users, by integrating content and functionality from both within the AltaVista Network and through external partners. Our primary focus is serving our users across the globe. Capitalising on our broad and distinctive offerings of innovative features and services, AltaVista delivers the ultimate Internet experience through (an) international network of (19) search oriented sites.

AltaVista's Business to Business Software and Services Division is a global leader in providing cutting edge search technology to e-commerce firms, portals and global enterprises.

AltaVista's focused approach is to continually build upon our proven foundation of technology leadership and results orientation. The company's overriding promise is to offer unmatched search services to the Web community through the integration of internally developed offerings, best of breed relationships and strategic acquisitions. Through our personalized local search services, we have created a global constellation of Web destinations to give users the best in relevant local search resources.

Good ideas, lightning fast and powerful hardware equipment, and a strange fascination with keeping track of email brought AltaVista out of DEC's Research lab and onto the Internet. In the spring of 1995, three DEC employees began talking about Digital's new Alpha 8400 (nick-named TurboLaser) computers over lunch. TurboLasers promised to run database software 100 times faster than the competition. Somewhere between bites of lunch, the idea of using TurboLasers to host a searchable full-text database of the Web was born.

Due to the lab's unusual fascination with keeping track of old email, a researcher had created a very precise email index to track bulletin board conversations posted over the past 10 years. The index was good at finding specific bits of information in the volumes of stored email. The researchers used this tool to settle fierce technical debates. This full-text search framework became the foundation of AltaVista - and one of the first search engines that continues to help people find specific information within the ever-expanding boundaries of the World Wide Web.

The idea for the name AltaVista originally came from a white board that hadn't been erased properly. The word Alto (of Palo Alto) was placed beside the word Vista and someone yelled out, 'How about Alto-Vista!' It then became AltaVista, meaning 'The view from above.'

Since the early days, other notable inventions to the engine include the first-ever multi-lingual searches on the Internet. We are also proud of Babel Fish - the Web's first Internet translation service that translates words, phrases, and entire Web sites online in Spanish, French, German, Portuguese and Italian. More recently, we launched Photo Finder, an image search technology. Other improvements include phrase detection, spell check, and natural language capabilities.

In January 1999, we became a wholly owned subsidiary of Compaq Computer Corporation (NYSE: CPQ). Compaq purchased Shopping.com in March. In August 1999, CMGI, Inc. (NASDAQ: CMGI) acquired 83 per cent of our outstanding stock from Compaq, and Shopping.com and Zip2 became a wholly owned subsidiary. With this combination, we now have a broad range of commerce and media content under the AltaVista domain. We have also introduced multimedia search capabilities and added a variety of customisable features to Microsoft Internet Explorer 5.

Today, we are rapidly expanding our global search services even further through the integration of each of our platforms and the constant introduction of new features and services. We remain committed to providing our users with the best search experience on the Web from a single source. As we develop new and better ways to reach our objectives and fulfill our users' needs, our 'view from above' promises to keep looking better and better.

Information services providers constitute a new and varied group. It could be argued that the oldest established members of this category are the libraries, which are still key organizations in modern societies. But if we concentrate on the idea of the coordination of modern information systems for other organizations as being characteristic of this group, then it still covers some interesting and varied enterprises.

Perhaps the longest-established type of firm are those which concentrate on developing bespoke (tailor-made) information systems for (mostly large) individual firms. Traditionally they are composed of systems analysts and programmers who first analysed customer needs, then helped specify the hardware to be bought, next wrote the code to be used, and finally supervised the installation and early operation of the new processes. The Yourdon consultancy in the USA would be a good example of this sort of operation.

With the development of relatively standardized PCs and sophisticated fourth-generation applications programs, such an approach is increasingly rare and often redundant. New firms have arisen and often focus on customizing a range of specialist software - perhaps a database product such as Oracle, or accounting or telesales products. In many cases hardware manufacturers such as IBM or software houses may run their own sales operations offering 'total solutions' to clients' problems. For the client, the choice of adviser may be a difficult one.

An independent consultant may be able to save money by suggesting combinations of products from different sources, but may be reluctant to accept responsibility if a part of the system is not actually supplied by them. An adviser tied to a particular hardware or software product may be 'free' and wholly responsible for its success or failure, but his or her solution may well be unnecessarily expensive and elaborate.

A relatively recently offered solution to this dilemma is that of the out-sourcer who provides and operates a complete system at a defined cost for the client. The oldest established members of this group are perhaps those offering specialist services such as payroll operations and security back-up. By amalgamating operations and developing specialist expertise, out-sourcers may well be able to provide services at much less cost than an 'in-house' group. From a client perspective, however, as we shall see, there are drawbacks such as the need to define in advance the level of service required and a strategic dependence on a third party outside their control.

INFORMATION SERVICES PROVIDER: EDS

EDS sees itself as the world's leading information technology Services Company. In the year 2000 its global turnover was $19.2 billion from 9,000 client organisations in 58 countries.

EDS supports 2.2 million desktops and 40,000 servers, and hosts websites for 750 clients. It processes 2.5 million ATM transactions a day and claims to be responsible for processing 11 billion daily transactions - equivalent to two transactions for everyone on earth.

Founded in 1962 as Electronic Data Systems, its early operations involved a handful of people processing clients' data by tapping into the idle time - usually at night - on other companies' mainframes. It now has 140,000 employees.

Its portfolio of services include Business Process Management, E solutions, Information Solutions and Management Consultancy. It stresses four themes in its relationships with customers:

- Collaborate in new ways: strategic alliances with customers and suppliers
- Continuous improvement: 'digitalise everything'
- Eliminate boundaries: operating anytime, anywhere
- Establish trust: 'gain customer intimacy, build digital wisdom and provide security and privacy'

An example of an EDS operation is Nova Scotia, Canada where EDS took over the mainframe computing operations of both the provincial government and the largest local telecommunications provider, MT&T, in a seven-year contract from 1992. Its data centre handles 350,000 interactive transactions per day in addition to 40,000 batch-processing jobs a month. All capital costs were met by EDS, which claims better service and lower costs have resulted.

AN INTENSIVE INFORMATION USER: HSBC BANK

The following information, largely derived from HSBC's Annual Report, stresses the growing importance of IT for an intensive information user:

HSBC (formerly the Hong Kong and Shanghai Banking Corporation) can fairly claim to be one of the largest banking and financial services organizations in the world. It is the successor to a merger between a Hong Kong-based bank and one of the largest UK banks - the Midland. HSBC had total assets of US$674 billion and shareholders' equity of US$46 billion by the end of 2000. With a headquarters in London, HSBC operates through long-established businesses in five regions: North America, Latin America, Europe, Hong Kong, and the rest of Asia-Pacific, including the Middle East and Africa. A world network of about 6,500 offices in 79 countries and territories clearly requires a sophisticated communications system. The group provides a wide range of financial services to personal and commercial clients.

HSBC sees the Internet as one of several exciting new media, to be incorporated as an integral part of its working. The bank has concluded that e-commerce will change the fabric of the financial services sector and sees it as a way of finding new customers all over the world and improving its services to existing customers. It intends to use e-commerce to reorganize the business so as to provide higher-quality customer services more efficiently.

HSBC will be able to link its customers to the full range of international services and manage their processing wherever it chooses, which the bank sees as a considerable competitive advantage. HSBC has adopted a 'clicks and mortar' strategy. This requires that customer Internet offerings must meet three criteria: customer needs and preferences come first; they must fit HSBC's existing distribution channels; and they must be multinational in scope.

Recently the group has been reorganizing its work for the e-age and putting in place some major components of such a strategy. In 2000, over US$2 billion was spent on technology, including a significant proportion on dot.com initiatives. HSBC aspires to be one of the first to provide customers with facilities through the Internet on a multigeographical, multi-product, basis.

IBM is developing an Interactive Financial Services (IFS) system for the bank which links in with the full range of customers' own technology: the Internet, interactive TV, mobile phones and other wireless modes of data transmission. IFS is designed to give HSBC's customers the freedom to access their finances where and when they wish. HSBC launched the UK's first nationally available TV banking service digital satellite provided by Sky in 1999. This has already attracted over 126,000 customers.

During 2000, HSBC has developed 'hsbc.com' as a brand name and a portal for its consumer services. By the end of 2000, Internet banking was available to HSBC customers in eleven of its businesses, including the United Kingdom, Brazil, Canada, the Hong Kong SAR, Singapore and the United States. Operations based in the Channel Islands serve Internet customers in 150 countries and territories. In 2000, in Brazil and France, HSBC began banking by mobile phone using WAP technology.

HSBC is a major supplier of collection, payment, account services and liquidity management throughout the world, so corporate customers and financial institutions can manage their cash efficiently on a worldwide basis. A key part of HSBC's strong market position in cash management is the flexibility of electronic delivery using Internet-enabled, file transfer or personal computers, as best suits the client concerned.

As long ago as 1989, HSBC's UK arm launched First Direct, the country's first complete 24/365 banking service by telephone. Despite the growth in competition, First Direct has continued to attract more customers. An Internet version of the service 'firstdirect.com', already has 270,000 clients.

Large-scale commercial and public sector users of information systems - intensive information users - cannot easily be distinguished from operations which are clearly part of the IT industry. Thus when the UK Department of Social Security out-sourced the operation of several of its major computer centres in a multi-million pound contract, the employees of these centres, now employees of EDS, were clearly part of the IT industry. It seems paradoxical to claim that they were not so before the out-sourcing, since their jobs were largely unchanged! Many parts of the financial services industry and the public sector, for instance, are now almost exclusively involved in the processing of information using modern technology.

They provide a major part of the career opportunities for IT graduates and are major investors in hardware and software. Similarly, as we have seen, many engineering manufacturing operations not only involve massive use of IT in their production processes but may also produce products - from cars to washing machines - with special purpose chips built into them.

The International Data Corporation has produced some interesting (if presumably very approximate) figures for the relative contribution of different types of firm to the economic value created by the IT; these give some idea of the relative financial importance of each.

THE STRUCTURE OF THE IT INDUSTRY

It will already be evident from the discussion of types of firm, and the individual case studies accompanying them that IT firms are closely related to each other. The question considered here is the sort of overall structure these relationships constitute and whether the industry structure is sufficiently competitive to safeguard the interests of consumers.

Moschella (1997) offers a useful and interesting overview of the past and likely future of the IT industry. Industrial evolution can be seen in terms of four waves of innovation, two of which have already happened, a third which is taking place now, the fourth being predicted by Moschella.

The first era of widespread commercial computing is, of course, that dominated by mainframe computers operated on behalf of corporate clients. From an industrial point of view it was an era in which, in the USA, IBM dominated the entire industry by supplying complete systems for the majority of large firms. It was said that 'no one ever got fired for buying IBM' in this period. In the US market there were, in fact, another seven fairly substantial system suppliers, whilst in some other countries, Britain being one; home-grown firms such as ICL achieved an almost comparable position to IBM in the USA.

At this stage major firms frequently designed software to suit their own hardware and often sold or leased direct to major customers, offering consultancy services in addition.

Smaller firms were often in a position of extreme dependency in offering a limited set of components or services to the major firms who sold 'bespoke' packages to large corporate customers.

Customers were frequently boxed into a relationship with a supplier, from which they could only escape with great expense and difficulty. This 'vertically integrated' market structure is characteristic of the early stages of new technologically innovatory products.

The first upset to this rather uncompetitive picture came with the development of mini-computer firms, a number of which developed relatively cheaper machines to run Unix operating systems thus offering buyers the possibility of changing machines without abandoning software or vice versa.

However, the massive change came with the development of the personal computer and the decision of IBM to out-source the supply of central processor units from Intel and an operating system (MS-DOS) from Microsoft. The availability of these key features of the IBM design to other 'original equipment manufacturers' (OEMs) was crucial to the emergence of a new industry structure. The competitive mass marketing of PCs to individuals, as well as to firms, has meant that IT provision has become much more a commodity sale rather than the provision of a bespoke service. The industry thus became horizontally divided into a series of markets, each dominated by different suppliers. Thus microprocessors were dominated by Intel, operating systems by Microsoft, local area networks by Novell, printers by Hewlett Packard, database management systems by Oracle, disks by Seagate, and so on.

A third wave of transformation in the industry has now clearly begun, with the increasing importance of networked computers - particularly through the operation of the Internet and private intranets. How this has happened is discussed in more detail later in this chapter, but from the point of view of industrial structure it clearly involves more, extremely powerful, corporate players. In particular three new types of firm must now compete, or form strategic alliances with, conventional computer firms. The first type of player is the telecommunications infrastructure provider, particularly the PTOs discussed earlier, but also cable television firms and the like.

The second are the manufacturers of consumer electronics products, which from mobile phones, through electronic games to digital televisions are increasingly overlapping in technology, function and markets with conventional PCs. Third are the multinational entertainment and news providers like the Murdoch Empire, Disney, and so on. Moschella suggests that at first, in the network-centric era telecom giants will dominate, but in the long run the providers of content will prevail. The 'governing principle' row is well worth some further immediate discussion here, however.

Herb Grosch's Law dates back to the 1940s and states that computer power increases as the square of the cost. This seems to favour the provision of bigger and more expensive (mainframe) machines since one computer that is twice as expensive as another will yield four times the processing power. It was this logic which prevailed in the 1960s and 1970s.

However, Gordon Moore, the founder of Intel, propounded the idea that semi-conductor performance would double every two years. This is a proposition that seems to have been confirmed by experience since the 1970s. The practical implications of this are the opposite of Grosch's Law because small 'commodity' machines are now developed much faster than mainframes on the basis of the latest high-power chips. Therefore it is often possible to replace an old expensive machine with a cheaper, more modern, one.

In addition, a series of PCs can often be networked together to form a 'virtual' larger machine at lower cost. This idea may be linked to the law associated with the name of Bob Metcalfe, the inventor of the Ethernet and founder of 3Com. He argued that whilst the cost of a network is linear (each extra machine costs roughly the same to add), the benefits are exponential (each extra machine brings in many more connections to the network - the larger the network the more connections).

Thus the cost of an extra machine on a three-machine network is (say) £1,000 and creates three extra communication links between existing machines and the new-comer - cost per extra link being £333.33. The cost of an extra machine on a 1,000-machine network is still £1,000 but creates 1,000 extra links at a cost of £1 per connection. This logic is clearly driving the creation of innumerable in-house and, still more, Internet links. The Internet clearly becomes more valuable the more potential customers are connected to it, but the cost of connection to it is static or declining as the technology becomes more established and demand increases.

What Moschella proposes as 'the Law of Transformation' is based on the observation of Professor Negroponte that there is a large contrast in the extent to which industries are based on 'atoms' or 'bits'. More physically based industries such as manufacturing might be thought to be less likely to be affected by changes in IT than information-based industries such as banking or government. However, in the three early stages of evolution in the information industries, somewhat surprisingly, this contrast has not been particularly apparent. Moschella argues that in the forth-coming content-centric stage of evolution, however, this contrast will be magnified.

He proposes a formula that suggests industries will be transformed in proportion to the square of the percentage of the value added by the industry, which is accounted for by bit-based information processing activities. Although Moschella's mathematical formulation of the law of transformation has an air of spurious precision, it does seem likely that some information-based activities like education and government have barely begun to be transformed to a fraction of their potential. The European Communications Council has recently published a stimulating report on the development of the Internet economy as a strategic challenge for business. The ten theses of this report give a good sense of fundamental changes that the Internet is helping to bring about.

A final recent development in terms of the economics of the IT industry which cannot be overlooked is the e-commerce 'dot.com' boom and crash which took place in the later years of the 1990s and burst in June 2000. This stock market speculative boom and bust was the latest in a series of speculations that have often related to new technology. Previous speculations include ones centring on exploring the South Seas, developing new breeds of tulips in Amsterdam, and the development of the railways in nineteenth-century Britain.

The common thread is that investment in what might be a useful if risky new area is over-hyped by speculators who benefit from selling on a rising market and naïve commentators carried away by the undoubted long-term prospects for the industry. People are drawn into investing in stocks in the hope of making profits, not from the venture (these being long-term) but from capital appreciation in the stocks rising in anticipation of profits not yet made. Thus numbers of 'dot.com millionaires' were created whose companies were still trading at enormous losses. Many - probably most - of these entrepreneurs, of course, sincerely believed their new ventures would be immensely profitable in the long run and some were amazed at their new-found instant wealth.

The scale of the investments and losses involved is difficult to document, but an article in the Washington Post estimates that US venture capitalists invested a total of $13 billion in telecommunications, Internet and software firms from January 1997 to September 2001. Companies such as EqualFooting.com Inc, Zona-Financiera.com Inc and Varsity-Books.com lost sums ranging from $30 to 69 million invested in them. Companies such as SciQuest - a company operating an on-line market in laboratory supplies - which did survive have found their share prices falling from a high of $80 to a price of around $1 in November 2001.

In Britain the Guardian estimated that the top 50 Internet entrepreneurs had accumulated personal fortunes of £1.3 billion over roughly the four years preceding October 1999. Many of these 'fortunes' represented the value of shares in companies whose price subsequently collapsed, but a follow-up article two years later revealed that most of them remained millionaires - if slightly poorer ones! The richest UK entrepreneur, Paul Sykes, had announced his intention of deserting the net scene in October 1999, did so, and consequently was still worth £425 million.

Unfortunately the e-commerce crash, when it came, affected more than just the companies whose only real assets were a handful of more or less skilled personnel, an Internet server and a marketing plan. The crash also hit companies with real and expensive assets (e.g. telephone cables, factories with state of the art technology) and thousands of ordinary professional and skilled employees, which needed to raise more capital for investment purposes.

A GLOBAL INDUSTRY

Information technology is now one of the most international of all industries. This is especially true of the production of PCs, as an examination of any PC assembled by an 'original equipment manufacturer' from any country will show. The operating system will almost certainly be American (from Microsoft). The microprocessor may well be from an American firm, but it may not necessarily be manufactured in the USA. CD-ROM drive and memory chips (DRAMs) may well come from Japan or Korea. The disk drive may originate from Singapore, monitor, keyboard and mouse from Taiwan.

As we saw earlier, however, by no means most of value added by the IT industry is from the manufacture of hardware. Distribution channels will frequently have a major local element. Telecommunications are normally dominated by national PTOs. Consultancy advice, out-sourcing and writing of specialist software will usually be provided by the local economy. British firms often write games software for Japanese consumer electronics manufacturers, and so on.

As content becomes more important then British publishers and Hollywood production firms may come to have a larger share in the predominantly English language market - although the dominance of English cannot be guaranteed as Chinese- and Spanish-speaking populations become richer and more involved in the global communications market.

The largest consumer market by far is the USA, followed by Japan and, if treated as a whole, Europe. Although Singapore, Taiwan and Korea and similar NICs (newly industrialized countries) have been able to compete in some specialist areas they lack large domestic markets for their products. Although Europe is an affluent market for IT products it has so far been unsuccessful in developing dominance in any one specialist area - except perhaps mobile phones (with the Finnish firm Nokia).

THE ECONOMY AND THE IT INDUSTRY

The IT industry's performance cannot be detached from the rest of industry, although, for much of the last 50 years, consumer electronics, television, video recorders and computers have helped to lead the growth of the world economy. In 2000/2001, conversely, a slump in computers and telecommunications has helped to generate a slowdown or recession in the world economy.

The industry depends on its customers and suppliers outside of the industry itself. It shares the same environment - e.g. trade unions, investment climate and resources, human resources, transport and communication facilities, wage rates. Porter (1990) argues that a crucial aspect of the competitiveness of national industries is precisely the availability of skilled labour, capital and relevant services (e.g. efficient telephone and electric ity supplies); the presence of a competitive supplier structure, a sophisticated domestic demand for the goods or services in question and a strong domestic competitive market within the industry. The success of other industries is crucially dependent on adoption of IT by them. Equally, investment in IT is capital investment by those other industries, and this is particularly sensitive to fluctuations in the economy.

THE GLOBAL INFORMATION MATRIX

Press reports increasingly speak of the 'information superhighway' as a dominant force in the modern world. Although an imprecise term, it does draw attention to the public availability of channels for the exchange of information across large parts of the globe through digital electronic networks. Increasingly this is being achieved by broadband technologies that permit multi-media exchanges involving voice and moving images, as well as the older-established use of text and graphics.

This should be distinguished from longer-established technologies such as the one-way broadcasting of information to mass audiences (of which satellite broadcasting is the latest example) and, less easily, from the use of older non-digital, narrow-band, electric communications technology such as (pre-ISDN) telephones, faxes and telexes.

Some writers speak of the 'wired society', but this may place too much emphasis on a technology that is already partially outdated by the development of private broadcast links and may be replaced by (e.g.) laser transmissions without cables. At present, however, the key technological expression of this is the development of fibre-optic cable links (although 'filaments' is perhaps a more accurate expression of their physical size).

With the development of ISDN (Integrated Services Digital Network) standards most of the advantages of broadband technology can be obtained via telephone cables. However, the cabling at present being installed mainly for TV entertainment purposes in many parts of the world does offer a broader-band link which might be used for other purposes - e.g. reading gas, electricity and water meters, security links to police stations, controls for area heating systems. In short, almost any number of WAN (wide area network) connections to computers elsewhere.

Technically the most impressive development in this direction so far is the development of the Internet. More capital has, however, been invested, so far, in converting the world's telephone networks to ISDN and to cabling for domestic entertainment purposes. In addition, numerous private global networks have been set up by multinational corporations and military alliances. Some of these are largely physically separate from public telephone/data networks and use their own dedicated satellite links and lines - 'superhighways' might be the most appropriate term.

THE GROWTH OF THE INTERNET

The Internet originated in the first experimental network of three computers financed by the US Department of Defense (c.1966). This developed into the ARPANET (first publicly demonstrated in 1972) and then the DARPANET which linked the major university research centres which had research contracts with the US Department of Defense (DoD).

Although financed by the DoD, the Internet was developed for the first decade or more almost entirely by university civilian researchers (mainly postgraduate students) as a 'pure' research project.

None the less, expenditure was justified as potentially allowing defence installations to be linked in case of enemy missile attack. The architecture of the Net, which has multiple connections and allows the network to continue even if individual lines or computers are down, reflects this. A separate defence network (MILNET) was hived off from the ARPANET in the early 1980s, which became the remote ancestor of the 'Star Wars' project to set up a computerized anti-missile-missile system.

As academic interest in the ARPANET grew, it was taken over by the National Science Foundation and used to link most major US universities (NSFNET). Overseas links were developed early - with University College London being a very early member of the ARPANET and researchers from it playing a part in defining its protocols. Other electronic networks, such as USENET, BITNET and, in the UK, JANET (the Joint Academic Network), have also developed with gateways allowing degrees of reciprocal access.

A distinction can be drawn between the Internet - a group of interconnecting networks running on IP/TCP (Internet protocols/transmission control protocols) - and the 'matrix', which is the sum total of WANs which largely interconnect to some extent and include many using commercial protocols such as IBM's SNA (System Network Architecture). A distinction should also be made between the Internet and intranets. The Internet is a publicly available series of interconnected networks, whilst intranets are private networks using the same protocols. Other protocols in use include, of course, OSI, favoured by European authorities and, nominally, the US government, and the X.25 etc. standards reflecting CCITT (telephone providers) requirements.

The growth of the matrix/Internet has undoubtedly been enormous, but is difficult to measure because of difficulties of definition, the decentralization of the matrix, and security devices that cloak the number of users of many nets. Gilster (1994) quotes estimates of 100 networks in 1985, 500 by 1989, 2,218 in 1990, 4,000 in 1991 and 16,000 plus by 1994. User numbers have been estimated at 25 million worldwide in 1994, with an estimated 419 million by December 2000 (NUA Internet Surveys, 2001).

Speeds have increased enormously to cope with increased traffic, with the original NSFNET backbone consisting of 6 nodes operating at 56 k-bits per second. By 1988 13 nodes were operating at 1.5 M-bits per second. By 1992 Advanced Network Services Ltd (alias IBM, plus two other companies) were operating a 45 M-bit per second service (i.e. 7,000 times faster than the original network) on behalf of NSFNET as well as a commercial version of the Internet (ANS CO+RE).

In fact the original networks were originally designed with remote logon chiefly in mind so that researchers at different universities could share expensive facilities. The potential for using the file transfer facility to develop a substitute for the post was only slowly appreciated. The most recent development - the World Wide Web - is an extension of the earlier idea of Bulletin Boards, which put files up for public access. With the development of graphic, video and sound file production and reception facilities, the distinction between viewing a computer file on a remote computer and viewing a television programme has been blurred. The distinctive feature of the WWW, however, is its interactivity - which means that a WWW site can be designed to respond to choices by the 'viewer' in a way impossible for conventional terrestrial television.

Tools such as gophers and the World Wide Web browsers enable information on almost any topic to be retrieved from a variety of sources worldwide. The development of the WWW and of user-friendly WIMP interfaces such as Windows has meant that the Internet has ceased to be a device accessible to a small, mainly academic, minority and has become a media available for mass communication. Millions of ordinary PC owners have gained access to the net in recent years. A new stage in the development of the web is its availability on much less expensive and more multipurpose devices such as mobile telephones and televisions. This is likely to lead over the next few years to affluent Western societies having a norm of at least one such device per household. The implications of this will be considered in later chapters.

INFORMATION ECONOMICS

Much is discussed today about advanced economies moving towards being an 'information economy'. The normal discussion presents a series of economic stages or eras, such as:

- Hunter-gatherer

- Agricultural
- Industrial
- Service or information.

The fundamental concept seems to be that, in terms of dominant activity (that is, the greatest part of the economy according to measures such as value of output, or number of people employed), there is an historical trend that progresses through these stages. Simple economies are in early stages, and advanced economies are in later stages. Each stage is characterized in part by the application of fundamentally new technology and human organization.

For example, Ward and Griffiths look at very recent history culminating in a Strategic Information Systems era. Skyrme discusses the 'networked knowledge economy'. Drucker discusses recent evolution from capitalism to a knowledge society. The notion of the information economy is a part of the broader question of the relationship between information and economy, so we shall first consider this question in terms of three fundamental areas of consideration:

1. Economic theory.
2. Macro-economic perspectives.
3. Micro-economic perspectives.

We shall then return to the definition of an 'information economy' and to the social and political implications of the concept, including the employment consequences of the widespread use of IT.

ECONOMIC THEORY

Classical economic theory in the West generally recognizes at least three factors of production: land, labour and capital. The key difference compared with Marxist economics lies in recognizing any factor other than labour (for example, is revenue from the sale of mineral resources to be treated as a return on the use of land as a factor of production, or is it to be treated as a return on the use of the labour used to extract and process the mineral?). A problem then lies in dealing with profit: is profit just a higher return to land, labour, or capital, or is it a return to some other factor of production such as enterprise or organization? This question is discussed in many well-known textbooks, such as Samuelson.

There has been some recent speculation that information should be treated as a factor of production for several reasons. A central theme of economic theory is the concept of perfect competition. In perfect competition it is argued that economic resources are allocated in an optimum way amongst the various members of the community through the market mechanism. An essential prerequisite for perfect competition is perfect knowledge of markets by buyers and sellers. Some writers use the term perfectly symmetric information to describe a situation of all players in a market having equal knowledge.

In game theory and information economics there is an important distinction between imperfect information and incomplete information. In markets, imperfect information exists when the behaviour of some market participants is not known. Incomplete information arises when all relevant factors are not known. The difference between imperfect and incomplete information is subtle but important. A company, particularly in a competitive market, is not likely to know everything about other players in the market. Some information may be kept secret by some players, or misleading information may be made available.

This leads to imperfect information. On the other hand, a company may not know all the factors relevant to a market. For example, an airline may think that other airlines are the principal competitors for business class travel. Perhaps some competition is really coming from electronic communications and the airline does not know how much electronic communication is a factor in deciding airline travel. In this case information is incomplete.

It is not often that the value of information is obtained just by transferring the ownership information (in other words, if it is moved from one company's database to another company's database). The value of information is realized by propagating it so that it can be used to affect some behaviour. Information by itself has no intrinsic value. The real value of information arises from changes arising from the information.

There is an important link here with strategic planning. Some critics argue that there is insufficient empirical evidence that having an articulated strategy is really useful to a firm. Information economics adds to that debate with a more sophisticated proposition that the usefulness of a business strategy is positively associated with the degree of information asymmetry in the market situation of the firm. For these several reasons, there are important links between information and economics.

MACRO-ECONOMICS

A macro-economic perspective concentrates on the relationships across economies as a whole. Some key macro-economic issues relating to information include:

- Employment: the proportion of the workforce involved in information or knowledge work.
- Output: how much of an economy's output can be defined as information or knowledge?
- Long-term relationships between information, economy, and underlying social normative drivers of economic activity.
- Relations between technology and economy as far as information and knowledge are concerned.

This kind of diagram is often used to justify an assertion that modern advanced economies are becoming information and knowledge economies. There are some potential fallacies in this line of thinking. People still eat and drink. There are more people. Therefore macro-economic output of the agricultural sector continues to rise. Fewer people are employed in agriculture now than in, say, the early twentieth century. These results have been achieved primarily through the application of technology in agriculture and the use of processes that require less labour.

Easier access to food and drink is also facilitated by the extensive deployment of transportation technology. People acquire and consume more material goods. There are more people. Therefore macro-economic output of the manufacturing sector continues to rise. As with agriculture, many parts of manufacturing have seen substantial productivity increases through the deployment of technology. So both agriculture and manufacturing remain enormously important sectors of the economy even if information is 'dominant'.

Some of the expansion of the information-work part of the economy has arisen not because there is more of that kind of work, but increasing 'out-sourcing' of services can gives the illusion of a fundamental macro-economic shift. For example, a manufacturing company that does all work such as accounting, design, marketing, finance, and law, in-house (such as a 'typical' nineteenth-century firm), will probably have all output and use of labour classified as manufacturing (if the primary output is manufactured goods).

Out-sourcing work such as accounting, marketing and public relations does not alter the amount of different kinds of work done. But if new firms of accountants and marketing and PR consultants arise as a result, there is the illusion that in macro-economic terms there is less manufacturing work and more information work.

- In the main classifications of the economic sector (agriculture, manufacturing, knowledge), there has been long-term increasing total output.
- Labour productivity has increased in terms of output per unit of labour.
- Capital to labour ratios has been increasing.
- Eventually there is a decline in the increase in capital productivity expressed in terms of the output per unit of capital input.

- The impact of IT change is essentially independent of whether it is directed to be labour or capital replacing; it depends more on the relationship between price and demand for the products or services outputs of the industries introducing the technology.

There are therefore long-term relationships between the pattern of employment and the deployment of technology. In simple terms, the Industrial Revolution would not have been possible if there had not been a sufficiently large available workforce freed by the deployment of agricultural technology and innovation. Similarly, increases in productivity in manufacturing have freed a large number of people to be available for services and information or knowledge work. Thus automation may have a short-term effect of increasing unemployment, but in the long term new activity acts to reduce the level of unemployment (OECD, 1987).

What we want, and what we believe, are results influenced to a very great extent by the information to which we have been subjected. Thus there are long-term relationships between information and norms about lifestyle. Lifestyle norms have a significant effect on demand for goods and services. Some people pursue more and more material goods as a matter of habit and desire; some have limits to their wants. Some macro-economic activity is driven by needs. Most is driven by wants. Wants are often the result of information and information processing. This long-term relationship between information, technology and normative economic drivers is discussed in Darnton and Giacoletto (1992).

MICRO-ECONOMICS

Micro-economics looks at problems at the level of the firm, or individual enterprise. Here there are different concerns about the interaction between information and economy. The key issues are:

- Production functions: for most goods and services the output can be generated in a variety of ways using different combinations of different factor inputs (land, labour, capital, organization, information);

- Costs of the different factors of production;
- Whether information assets exist in the sense of having value or being able to support a future stream of income;
- How can the benefits of IT be evaluated? (What is the return on investment?)

Information is an important ingredient in establishing prices and revenue. Demand for factors of production is demand derived ultimately from what customers want, and decisions those in enterprises take about production functions. As far as information is concerned, the special economic properties listed earlier indicate that it is a very difficult factor to replace. However, information and IT are used in many cases to replace other factors of production.

IT has clearly automated many kinds of information work, thus replacing labour. IT, when embedded with other technologies, has been able to replace much capital (for example, computer-supported numerical controlled machines can reduce the need for a larger number of dedicated machines). The use of IT to relocate information work, or to disperse it, enables the substitution of expensive real estate by less expensive real estate.

Choices between factors of production may be made purely on cost grounds, but they may also be taken on the premise of having greater control over processes. Thus the use of IT in some cases may be more expensive than the equivalent labour costs, but greater control can be exercised over machines than over people. Computers do not react against an authoritarian management style; but people might. On a more positive note, more IT may result in more flexible processes.

The value of information assets per se can be judged from various perspectives. The value of an enterprise is greater with the information assets than without. The earliest example of this, recognized widely, is the valuation of an enterprise in terms of its tangible assets, plus an additional sum for 'goodwill' - this is generally the willingness of customers to return to the enterprise and knowledge of customers and their behaviour.

Information assets may be deployed to produce a future stream of income. For example, a lawyer familiar with legal principles and practice can use that knowledge to generate an income even though the knowledge in the lawyer's head may have no other extrinsic value. In other cases, a specific information asset, such as copyright or licence rights in computer programs, may have extrinsic capital value and in addition, the enterprise may be able to use it to generate income from (say) licence fees.

In non-monetary terms information and knowledge may be valued because the individual concerned has high regard for that kind of information. For example, a book collector may place a high value on a rare book. (Rarity is a function of how many other people want the item in question, compared with what is available.) There has been great difficulty in establishing clear, unambiguous methods for evaluating the returns available from many IT investments.

Where this can be done is usually where there is a clearly defined project of factor replacement when all costs and outputs are identifiable. For example, it may be possible to estimate the return on investment of replacing a set of manual typewriters by a computer-based word-processing system. In many cases, IT investments take on the nature of infrastructure investments and these are notoriously difficult to evaluate in terms of return on investment. Thus some writers have focused on the difficulty of making simple general associations between IT investment and enterprise performance, while others have focused on the need to consider the evaluation of benefits in much broader terms than purely financial.

Information is an essential ingredient to support more sophisticated approaches to pricing. Perhaps the most traditional approach to pricing is cost-plus, where the costs of production at a certain level of output are calculated, and something is added for profit. Beyond that, there are other possible approaches, all dependent on the availability of the right information:

- Opportunity cost: pricing is determined by alternative opportunities for revenue generation which have been foregone;
- Market value: prices are determined by 'what the market will stand';
- Value pricing: prices are determined by the value of the goods or services to the buyer (ideally, in economic theory, the greatest profit will be achieved if every price is set individually between each buyer and seller).

As was briefly discussed earlier, human societies can be seen as having gone through four stages: hunter-gatherer, agricultural, industrial and service or information (or post-industrial). These will now be considered in more detail in terms of the dominant method of production, styles of living, distribution of power and their associated information technologies.

Economists frequently describe sectors of the economy in terms of primary (extractive), secondary (manufacturing), tertiary (services) or quaternary (information). Clearly all economies, even the simplest 'tribal' economies, include all four types of activity, but the tendency over time is for activities to become more specialized and the balance between them to shift from primary up the scale to first, secondary, then to tertiary and perhaps finally to quaternary activities.

Thus in both hunter-gatherer and agrarian economies the main economic activities - first of all, gathering wild plant products, hunting wild animals and fishing, then farming planted crops and domestic animals - are mainly concerned with extracting raw materials from the earth. In the industrial era the craft skills used for manufacturing on a small scale in domestic establishments are replaced by factory mass production systems which come to employ the bulk of the labour force and produce most of the wealth in the economy.

In the information era, although farming and industrial manufacturing continue to be major economic activities, research, education, design, finance and marketing activities employ more personnel and are seen as the crucial activities 'adding value' in the supply chain.

Clearly, as economies shift from hunter-gatherer to post-industrial the standard of living will rise from conditions in which people exist on the margins of existence, through subsistence farming, to an increasing affluence as industrial economies develop. In information economies the optimistic prediction is made that everyone will achieve a high and stable standard of living with increasing amounts of leisure for all. Some geographical contrasts between these historical eras are worth remarking upon. In hunter-gatherer societies tiny populations are nomadic - shifting with the availability of edible foodstuffs. In small settled and rural communities of agricultural economies there is relatively little mobility - though some long-distance trade may occur in luxury goods.

There is no distinction between home and workplace, with farmer and labourers, or craftsman and apprentices, living and working together. In industrial economies, large urban populations work in one place and commute daily to work. There is more travel and migration than is found in agricultural systems. In the information era, in the long term, it is possible that an enormous global community is no longer restricted by geography in that a global communication system makes the dominant information-related type of work possible anywhere.

Corresponding to each economic system, as Marx and Engels argued, those in power in the community (the elite) are likely to differ. Thus hunter-gatherer societies are led by those few older members of the tribe who survive and are respected as the repositories of the wisdom of the group. (Thus information leads to power?) In agrarian societies the land is the source of wealth so that the major landowners tend to dominate socially and politically. With industrialization comes the political and social triumph of capitalists - the owners of the factories that are the key to the wealth of the economy.

It is argued by writers such as Bell that in the post-industrial era the new elite will be the 'technocrats' and managers who understand and can control the scientific and technical information which is now the real basis of wealth. In each era human beings' relationship to their environment under-goes a radical shift. At first humans are parts of the ecological system - one more species competing for survival in a harsh landscape beyond their control. With the development of agriculture, however, over centuries humanity remakes the landscape and comes to control which species they are prepared to cohabit with. A process accentuated by industrialization where, in a still shorter timescale, industrial pollution can render whole areas virtually uninhabitable.

It is to be hoped that in the post-industrial era, with a greater understanding of ecological variables, deliberate conservation of a multiplicity of habitats for all the species of the planet may prevail. Each historical era can be seen as having its distinctive technology. Hunter-gatherer societies are characterized by a limited range of tools mainly made or even improvised by the users (spears, sticks to knock down high-growing fruit, etc.). In agricultural economies specialized craftsmen such as blacksmiths or carpenters may develop quite sophisticated human- or animal-powered tools.

The distinctive feature of industrial economies is the development of other sources of power and the use of mass manufacturing techniques in factories. Water power was soon replaced by steam power in the early Industrial Revolution. Later on, of course, the internal combustion engine and electricity became increasingly important. The distinctive technology of the information economy is of course the digital electronic computer. Whilst digital information technology can be seen as the defining characteristic of this latest era of economic development, earlier eras too had characteristic technologies of communication. Hunter-gatherer societies probably developed through a capacity to use speech; other means of communication, such as smoke signals and cave painting, were either economically or culturally significant too.

Many agricultural societies developed writing and the use of mathematical technologies such as the abacus. In ancient Egypt and elsewhere, such communications were probably important in maximizing agricultural production and certainly were useful politically. In industrial economies printing was undoubtedly associated with the spread of scientific knowledge and technological innovation. Broadcasting has helped to spread new patterns of mass consumption in many economies. We have already discussed at length, and will develop further, the key role of computers and global networks in the current era.

Related to the issue of information technology is what IT is being used to convey: knowledge. If we assume that early societies were like the preliterate societies of today or yesterday, which have been studied by social anthropologists, then the most important type of knowledge can be assumed to be tribal custom - the inherited wisdom of the ancestors of the group. In more sophisticated agrarian societies the most important and certain traditional knowledge was often theological. In a few societies, traditions of scholarship were developed which often included practical and legal insights as well as theology.

The Greeks and the Romans also developed methods of philosophical inquiry, which can be seen as the ancestors of the modern natural and social sciences. Round about the time of the Industrial Revolution philosophical thought took a more rationalist and empirical turn and the new physical sciences began to contribute greatly to the rapid development of technology. It may be argued that in the post-industrial era rational techniques of inquiry are being increasingly applied, not only to technological but also to social problems. Modern professions such as economists, systems analysts, operational research specialists, market researchers, etc. can be seen as developing essential expertise which must form the basis of informed social decision-making whether by managers in industry or by politicians.

The power of these 'technocrats' - expert users of the massive databases increasingly made available by the new technology - can be seen to be inevitably increasing as we move further into the twenty-first century. It makes a formidable case for the major significance of the widespread adoption of modern information and communication technology as a major turning point in the history of human society. However, there are a number of critical objections to such a thesis, some of which were discussed earlier.

One major area of objection may be to the implication that such a scheme involves a rather nineteenth-century view of the inevitable progress of mankind as the result of technological and economic innovation. The author certainly would not accept that there is necessarily any moral, aesthetic or cultural superiority of the later stages in this process of change. Certainly from anthropological and historical descriptions some hunter-gatherer or agrarian societies may well be happier places than many industrial ones. It is clear, too, from the historical record that there is no inevitability to the transition from one type of society and economy to the next.

Also there are many theories about the causes of such changes, none of which can be unequivocally regarded as established. However, it is worth suggesting that there is some sort of 'fit' between different types of society, economy and technology, as described in this account. Another obvious area of controversy centres around the final post-industrial or information stage of economy and society. Have we (or perhaps the United States and Japan) already entered it - or is it the likely next stage of development? Are some of the descriptions of the likely impact of IT on society over-optimistic and utopian? In particular does such a society represent a real break in the economic and social realities of capitalist industrial economies?

These are large questions which cannot be finally resolved in a book of this kind, but we will return to some of them in our final chapter. In any event, there is no denying the immense importance of IT in contemporary society, whatever its exact role in terms of causation.

DEFINING AND MEASURING THE INFORMATION ECONOMY

Earlier in the chapter we touched upon the difficulty of defining what an 'information economy' was. It is worth considering briefly how it can be defined and measured and applies this to some contemporary states. An early treatment (1986) of this is a report by the Organization for Economic Cooperation and Development (OECD).

All of these occupations dc deal with information in some sense (but not necessarily with modern digital information technology), and using such definitions the report showed that the number of information workers had been increasing rapidly in developed countries since the Second World War. On this basis the USA certainly now has a majority of information workers in its employed population. But somewhat paradoxically such figures show a massive growth in 'information workers' (mainly those in semi-skilled clerical operations) before computers were widely employed in American industry.

Miles (1990) employs an alternative and perhaps more convincing approach to the definition of the information economy by focusing on the use of micro-electronic silicon 'chips'. For him the 'core' of the information economy is represented by producers of such chips, whilst the 'heart' consists of information technology producers and providers such as those involved in telecommunications and computer manufacturing, computer services (software) and communication services (VANS - value added network services). The rest of industry, he suggests, could be assessed for the degree to which it makes intensive use of IT by measuring the extent to which it purchases.

In principle this seems a more convincing method of measuring the spread of the use of IT throughout modern industry, but unfortunately the author knows of no definitive figures available on this basis. In the long run, any such attempt is bound to be a rather rough and ready exercise since, for instance, as chips become more powerful the employment of one chip may represent a different degree of involvement with the technology. Equally, using many computers to word-process invoices represents less dependence on the technology than using one computer to control a whole set of production processes.

IT AND EMPLOYMENT

One of the key variables in this discussion has been the extent to which people are employed in occupations affected by IT. But what is the impact on total employment of the use of computers? Here we are considering three related topics. First, what an a priori economic analysis would lead us to expect the impact of innovations involving microprocessor technology to be. Second, we relate IT to the known causes of unemployment. Third, we consider some relevant empirical evidence. Here we are considering primarily the impact of IT on the quantity of employment; at a later stage we shall consider the impact of IT on the quality of employment available.

An economic analysis might appropriately begin at the micro (firm) level with a conventional but useful distinction between process and product innovation. In the former the innovation is used as a part of the production process to produce an unchanged product; in the latter a new or improved product (or service) involving the technology is developed. These would appear to be likely to have different employment implications.

As far as process innovation is concerned we would appear to have a conventional case of capital investment, in which if it is assumed that the price and quantity of the good to be sold and the materials employed is unchanged then the only rational justification for the investment involved must be a lowering of labour costs, probably involving job losses. This is the gloomy assumption upon which predictions of substantial job losses from IT are based.

Note, however, that there are alternatives for firms involved in process innovation - e.g. if more goods can be sold (even at reduced prices) the same (or even increased) total labour costs may be justified as the labour cost per unitof good sold is thereby reduced. The product innovation case, conversely, would appear to have positive implications for the predicted demand for labour since a new product must surely produce a new demand for labour by the entrepreneur concerned, whilst an improved product would only be marketed if it produced greater profits and would be therefore likely to lead to an increased demand for labour.

At the macro (whole economy) level, unfortunately, it cannot be assumed that these findings can be automatically applied, since, for instance, process innovation by efficient firms may lead to the collapse of less efficient rivals (and the loss of their workers' jobs) whilst increased demand for the a new product (e.g. video cassette recorders) may lead to a loss of demand for rival older products (e.g. outings to the cinema).

Of the three major types of unemployment usually recognized by economists (frictional, structural and demand deficiency) the last two seem most likely to be of importance here. However, frictional unemployment may be slightly reduced by the availability of improved techniques of data retrieval and communication which can be used on behalf of, or by, the unemployed so as to match job vacancies and applicants.

Structural unemployment may result from either type of innovation as the new processes require (or appear to require) different types of labour from those made redundant. For example, older male welders are lost and young female data processing staff are demanded, or the products are produced in areas like south-east England or Japan where relatively high levels of employment are already found, whilst areas such as Tyneside (dominated by traditional declining product-producing industries) register high and increasing labour surpluses.

However, it is worth emphasizing, the major importance of the overall level of demand, in that, as we have seen, in circumstances when overall demand is buoyant, process innovation is likely to lead to an expansion of production and a richer society; product innovation, similarly, should mean that new products will be consumed in addition to the old rather than substituted for them.

Many of the gloomier predictions of the impact of IT have been based on a neglect of the economic realities of investment considerations. Technological possibilities are frequently mistaken for economic inevitabilities, as Graves points out. Graves himself gives a long and gloomy list of doomed occupations, ranging from teachers in higher education, through postmen and check-out girls to transport workers. This sort of pessimism led Jenkins and Sherman (1979) to predict a loss of 23 per cent in the labour force between 1978 and 2003. It is amusing to look at some of the older works in the field and note the extent to which predictions have failed.

Post Office mails business continues to mushroom (on word-processed junk mail), despite some decades of prediction that electronic mail was about to replace it. Cash-less purchasing, which according to Finn (1984) was to have paid for its installation costs by 1988, was only introduced into local Sainsbury's in 1990, and so on. Whilst something like the job loss predicted by Jenkins and Sherman occurred in the UK between 1978 and 1983, it is clear that it was overwhelmingly the result of a loss of overall demand in the economy, not of technological innovation.

Earlier in the chapter we saw some statistics (frequently quoted in connection with 'post-industrial' or 'information' society controversies) which show a considerable relative increase in the 'information-linked' and service industries apparently at the expense of manufacturing, but it is worth pointing out that much of the growth of these sectors has predated the application of microprocessor technology to them, whilst the decline of manufacturing (and agriculture in the developed world) is clearly linked to very heavy capital investment.

In the jumble of somewhat conflicting assertion it is refreshing to find some clear, if limited, empirical evidence in the shape of the regular PSI surveys of British manufacturing industry. At first sight they appear to show a wide-scale adoption of microprocessor technology accompanied by very little reduction in employment (estimated at a total loss of 121,000 in the whole of British manufacturing industry between 1981 and 1985). However, the authors do caution us that only an estimated 12.5 per cent of manufacturing processes have yet been even partially 'automated', and that the larger job losses are associated with the more intensive users.

Other findings are somewhat unexpected - for instance, on a regional basis there is no perceptible southern bias, and the expected contrast between product and process users fails to materialize. In addition to the authors' cautions on their data we might add that only 10 per cent of the workforce are employed in manufacturing, and that job losses are direct ones within the plants concerned whilst a greater job loss may have occurred amongst rival plants which have not automated.

More generally we might add that British manufacturing industry appears to have 'raised' productivity in recent years, not by investing in microtechnology but by eliminating 'uneconomic' plants and using labour more intensively. Japanese, American and newly industrialized country entrepreneurs may have, wisely, followed a different strategy, with serious potential consequences for British employment figures in the UK's exceptionally open economy.

4

Information Technology on Leadership Opportunities for Women

Advances in information technology (IT) are providing leadership opportunities for women both in upper and middle management. This chapter aims to fill the gap in the literature concerning the effects of IT on these leadership opportunities by examining IT's potential as a leveler of the corporate playing field, facilitating the entry of women into the upper ranks of management and allowing those in middle management to emerge as leaders in decision-making groups. Specifically, the explosive growth of talent-driven Internet-related businesses has opened up opportunities in upper management for women, while the very nature of the Internet and computer-mediated communication (CMC) has the potential for increasing the opportunities for emergent leadership by women within middle management.

Four interrelated factors are suggested as to why Internet companies are playing the role of the "great leveler" of leadership opportunities in upper management: (a) the demand for qualified top managers; (b) the nonexistence of an "old boy" network; (c) the existence of diversified, mixed gender personal networks; and (d) an organizational culture open to diversity, which is typical of Web-related firms. Two factors are suggested as enablers of leadership emergence by women in middle management in decision-making groups: (a) technology-based information accessibility, and (b) potentially increased participation in decision-making through CMC.

Advances in information technology (IT) are providing leadership opportunities for women both in upper and middle management. Well-developed bodies of research exist on women and leadership and on IT and gender. Moreover, there have been recent studies on leadership in computer-mediated work groups. Nevertheless, there is a gap in the literature concerning the effects of IT on leadership opportunities for women.

This chapter aims to fill this gap by examining IT's potential as a leveler of the corporate playing field, facilitating the entry of women into the upper ranks of management and allowing those in middle management to emerge as leaders in decision-making groups. The relationship between IT and leadership opportunities for women deserves exploration in light of two significant trends: the existence of the "glass ceiling" that prevents women from advancing to top management and the lack of equal decision-making participation of women in middle management despite their equal representation within these middle ranks. The explosive growth of talent-driven Internet-related businesses has opened up opportunities for women in upper management, while the very nature of the Internet and computer-mediated communication (CMC) has the potential for increasing the opportunities for emergent leadership by women within middle management.

NEW OPPORTUNITIES FOR WOMEN IN UPPER MANAGEMENT

The dearth of women in the ranks of upper management is a reality of corporate life, with women encountering an invisible barrier to advancement, which has been commonly referred to as the "glass ceiling", to the extent that discrimination accounts for women's underrepresentation in the ranks of leaders and managers, women's credentials and performance are not fairly evaluated. The same leadership behaviors, when performed by a woman, may be viewed less favorably than they are when performed by a man.

A number of interrelated reasons have been advanced for the "glass ceiling" barrier, including a patriarchal social system, organizational gender composition, and a preference for similar colleagues. In a patriarchal system, where men dominate women, society regards men as having higher social status than women, resulting in the devaluation of women's accomplishments and contributions.

Women's presence in top management positions violates the societal norm of men's higher status and superiority to a greater extent than women's presence in lower-level management positions. This norm may be perpetuated by direct discrimination on the part of the dominant group of males against women who violate the norm by seeking high-level positions.

According to Cohen et al. (1998), the hiring and promotion of managers is a function of organizational gender composition. In firms where top management is overwhelmingly male, this societal norm of male superiority will be reinforced. However, Cohen et al. found that in organizations where some top management posts are already filled by women, other women are more likely to be hired for or promoted to senior positions. The similarity hypothesis maintains that a major determinant of interpersonal attraction between individuals is the degree to which they are similar. Thus, individuals will favorably evaluate those who are perceived to be like themselves. Kanter (1977), applying this notion to the hiring practices of top management, posits that women face an entry barrier to upper management positions in male-dominated hierarchies precisely because they are women: predominantly male upper management simply views women as different.

Powell offers this explanation as to why the proportion of women in upper management has remained relatively small as opposed to the proportion of women in middle management, which is roughly equal to that of men.

The forces driving the increase in the proportion of women in management overall have had less effect on the proportion of women in management. The higher the position within managerial ranks, the less the importance of "objective" credentials that women may acquire, such as education.... As a result, women's increased educational attainment, which represents a change in the quality of the labour supply, has had a greater effect on hiring and promotion into entry-level management positions than into those at the top.

The commercialization of the Internet, whose advent has given rise to a proliferation of Internet companies, has opened up new opportunities for women to break through the "glass ceiling" and lead or manage corporations. These Web-related firms are the corporate frontier of the New Economy, where women are finding greater leadership opportunities than in traditional Old Economy companies. According to one research firm, women held 45 percent of senior management positions and 6 percent of chief executive posts at venture capital-financed Internet companies in 1999, as opposed to 21 percent and 4 percent, respectively, in 1998.

Recently, a growing number of news reports in the financial press and business pages have concerned the appointment of women to top management posts at Web-related firms, including the positions of chief executive and president. For example, Heidi Miller left her position as chief financial officer at Citigroup and joined Priceline.com, the Internet retailer, where, as part of a management triumvirate, she will oversee finance and strategy.

As reported in a New York Times article, "Ms. Miller says that Priceline offered something she savored: `a seat at the table' - the power to run a business, an opportunity that might elude her as a woman in mid-career at the layered life that is Citigroup". Similarly, Patricia Fili-Krushel, quit her position as ABC network president to become president and chief executive of the consumer division of Healtheon/ WebMD, an Internet health care company.

Another news item relates how after 21 years in the magazine publishing business, Wenda Harris Millard was tapped for the position of executive vice president at DoubleClick, a firm that tracks consumer usage of the Internet. In a Wall Street Journal interview, Judith Spreiser discusses her leaving Sara Lee Corp., where she was food division CEO, in order to pursue "a fabulous opportunity" at Transora, an Internet business-to-business food and consumer-product cooperative, where she will assume the post of chief executive, making her Transora's first leader.

A recent issue of Employment Review Online provides a partial listing of successful women leaders - most of whom hold the positions of both president and CEO - at Internet companies, including eBay, Exodus Communications, iVillage, and Pets.com. Four interrelated factors may be suggested as to why Internet companies are playing the role of the "great leveler" of leadership opportunities: (a) the demand for qualified top managers; (b) the nonexistence of an "old boy" network; (c) the existence of diversified, mixed gender personal networks; and (d) an organizational culture open to diversity, which is typical of Web-related firms.

THE DEMAND FOR QUALIFIED TOP MANAGERS

In Web-related companies, operating in a fast-paced, results-oriented environment, where swift decision-making is necessary to accommodate innovation, there is a great demand for top managers with talent. This need for talent makes the selection of individuals for top management posts to be on the basis of merit without regard to gender. Hence there are leadership opportunities for well-qualified women, who are expected to flourish in senior management and chief executive positions. For example, there are leadership opportunities for women in e-commerce because many women have backgrounds in management and marketing, two areas that are especially crucial to e-commerce.

THE NONEXISTENCE OF AN OLD BOY NETWORK

One factor contributing to the "glass ceiling" phenomenon has been reliance on the "old boy" network for recruiting and hiring top management. This informal group of men in leadership positions - who are connected to each other professionally and socially - has served both as a source of referrals and as a pool from which traditional firms have drawn their senior managers and chief executives. As a result, women have been excluded from the ranks of upper management. However, at the relatively new, untraditional Internet companies, with their egalitarian views and positive attitudes toward diversity, the environment has not been hospitable for the development of "old boy" networks. As such, Web-related firms have opened the door to a more heterogeneous top management, where women are welcome.

THE EXISTENCE OF DIVERSIFIED, MIXED GENDER PERSONAL NETWORKS

Replacing "old boy" networks as sources of referrals and talent are more diversified, mixed gender personal networks, consisting of former and present colleagues, classmates, friends, mentors, and proteges. These personal networks are responsible for the phenomenon known as the "Pied Piper" effect, which occurs when a talented top manager, having a loyal following of co-workers, leaves one company for another, and the co-workers follow - sometimes all of them switching simultaneously to the other firm as a team. "And the prime movers are the A-rated leaders at the heart of these networks who can get others to follow them into uncharted territory". Thus, these networks are an especially rich source of diversified talent, a source from which talented women leaders can be drawn.

AN ORGANIZATIONAL CULTURE OPENS TO DIVERSITY

Because of their relative newness, Internet companies are not burdened with the cultural biases that have shaped stereotyped negative perceptions regarding the leadership abilities of women. It is these negative perceptions that have contributed to the "glass ceiling" in traditional firms. By virtue of being nontraditional and valuing diversity, Web-related firms have welcomed women to top leadership positions.

Moreover, the presence of women in top leadership posts in an Internet company makes it more likely that additional women will join them in upper management. The reason for this "snowball" effect is that with male incumbents not dominating the ranks of senior management, there is no discriminatory preference for men. According to Rosener, "[w]omen managers who have broken the glass ceiling in medium-sized, nontraditional organizations have proven that effective leaders don't come from one mold."

Women today constitute 50 percent of middle management. As previously noted, research has suggested that these proportions are the result of educational and other "objective" credentials carrying greater weight for middle management positions than for the ranks of upper management. Despite their roughly equal representation in middle management, women do not participate equally with men in group decision-making. Research has indicated that there is a direct relationship between the rate of participation in group discussions and leadership emergence. Thus, within middle management decision-making groups, leadership by women is lagging.

IT has the potential for reversing the state of affairs. Specifically, two factors are suggested as enablers of leadership emergence by women in middle management decision-making groups: (a) technology-based information accessibility, and (b) potentially increased participation in decision-making through computer-mediated communication (CMC).

TECHNOLOGY-BASED INFORMATION ACCESSIBILITY

INFORMATION SHARING AND POWER

The Internet makes information and knowledge, which are sources of power, accessible to all, thereby empowering employees and middle managers, including women. The variety and comprehensive nature of the information available on the Web combined with powerful search engines that facilitate access to such information allow one to quickly and easily gain expert knowledge in a given area. An individual with such knowledge can thereby wield considerable influence over colleagues through the exercise of expert power, which results from having some distinct knowledge or skill. Through such Web-obtained expert power, women middle managers in decision-making groups can influence others and emerge as leaders.

Women managers are especially good at sharing information and knowledge with others. Such sharing is vital for an organization's success because it allows appropriate personnel to gain a complete and accurate picture of the organization, including its customers and competitors. With the advent of the Internet and the vast amounts of information that are available on it, the sharing of information can be easily accomplished on a large scale and with a minimum expenditure of time. For example, the identical e-mail message, as well as information obtained on the Internet, may be distributed to multiple recipients simultaneously. This sharing propensity of women managers allows for the sharing of Web-based information, thus ensuring that information that is available and accessible is, in fact, disseminated.

The sharing by women managers of such information plays an important role in the development of strong interpersonal relationships and in the creation of a loyal following "by signaling to coworkers... that they are trusted and their ideas respected", enabling women managers in decision-making groups to emerge as leaders within these groups and to increase their "capacity to influence the attitudes, values, or behaviors of others". Thus, it is suggested that this sharing of information may result in referent power, which is power based on strong interpersonal ties that develop from the respect, liking, and admiration of others within the organization.

According to French and Raven, referent power is an extremely effective source of social influence. The sharing of information also results in expert power, which, as discussed above, exists when one possesses some special knowledge or expertise. However, whereas one can exercise expert power over others only so long as one possesses more knowledge than they do, referent power will endure as long as one retains the respect, liking, and admiration of others and is thus more likely to result in a loyal following.

DECENTRALIZATION OF DECISION-MAKING AND LEADERSHIP OPPORTUNITIES

In today's global business environment, where flexibility, reduced costs, swift decision-making, and quick response to market conditions and competitive pressures are essential for survival and growth, an increasing number of organizations are harnessing IT to transform themselves into nimbler, more efficient, and flatter entities. In these flatter organizations, IT - Internet, intranet (an individual firm's private network using Internet technology), and extranet (two or more private interconnected networks using Internet technology) - is used to disperse information throughout the firm, thereby eliminating layers of unnecessary managers and decentralizing decision-making.

IT has the potential for empowering the remaining middle managers, both men and women, by enabling them to obtain information heretofore available only to upper management and thus make decisions that were formerly the province of the latter. The trend toward flattening organizational structures has been characterized by Fulk and DeSanctis (1995) as a shift away from social rationalization (hierarchical mechanisms) to technological rationalization (electronic communication).

This reduction of layers of hierarchy is made possible by the widening of the span of control (the number of subordinates a supervisor controls), a process in which IT plays a critical role by, among other things, assuming management's coordinating function, allowing for asynchronous communication over geographically dispersed locations so that individuals need not be available at the same time, and permitting the storage and retrieval of information from shared data bases. Thus, the decentralization of decision-making in flat organizations results in leadership opportunities for middle managers, half of whom are women.

POTENTIALLY INCREASED PARTICIPATION IN DECISION-MAKING THROUGH COMPUTER-MEDIATED COMMUNICATION

A driving force for the full and equal participation of women in group decision-making within corporations - potentially advancing their emergence as leaders within these groups - has been computer-mediated communication (CMC). The latter term refers to a variety of computer systems and software that employ computer networks to promote and expedite communication and includes e-mail, computer conferencing, and, relevant for our purposes, group support systems (GSS).

GSS, also known as groupware, is an interactive computer-based information system that supports and structures group interaction and decision-making, including idea generation and problem solving. GSS is, thus, "a set of techniques, software and technology designed to focus and enhance the communication, deliberations and decision making of groups". Many major firms have adopted various kinds of GSS software to assist in group decision-making. For example, Domino's Pizza has recently selected Centra 99, LensCrafters has chosen GroupWise, and Lucent's Bell Laboratories is currently using Rear View Mirror.

A key feature of GSS is anonymity, or anonymous interaction, whereby group members interact with each other and put forth ideas without their identities being disclosed. This anonymity feature is especially important because it enables ideas to "be evaluated on their inherent worth and not on the reputation or rank of their proposers". In traditional face-to-face (FTF) mixed gender groups, men have tended to emerge as leaders more frequently than women. This finding has been explained by reference to expectation states theory, a social psychological theory which posits that group members will tend to evaluate their fellow members on the basis of their stereotypical performance expectations, which are influenced by external status characteristics.

When gender is treated as a status characteristic, the theory predicts that because society regards men as having higher status than women, the task contributions of men will be regarded as more valuable than the contributions of women. The devaluation of women group members' performance and contributions has resulted in the decreased participation of women, thereby hindering their emergence as group leaders.

It is suggested that in computer-mediated groups using anonymity-featured GSS, gender will be eliminated as a status characteristic because the differentiating gender cues will not be communicated. Thus, anonymity allows for the evaluation of ideas without the distorting influence of gender, equalizing male-female participation rates and enabling women members to emerge as leaders in initially leaderless groups. While anonymity in GSS results in the absence of gender cues, individual linguistic features (e.g., language, grammar, repeated phrases) will, to a large extent, serve to distinguish the various unidentified group members. In this way, an individual member's participation will be recognized while remaining anonymous, with each member having an equal opportunity to emerge as a leader without regard to considerations of gender.

Although research has demonstrated that gender differences in emergent leadership disappear over time as group members interact with each other, women will have the opportunity to emerge as leaders even in newly constituted computer-mediated groups. This is so because the anonymity feature of GSS should neutralize the reluctance of women in mixed gender groups to participate in decision-making, the participation rate being positively related to leadership emergence.

Apparently due to the proprietary nature of the data, no published case studies exist for the support of the proposition that the use of GSS by middle management decision-making groups facilitates the emergence of women leaders within these groups. Surprisingly, neither are there any reports of experimental studies testing this hypothesis. However, as previously noted, the scholarly literature is highly suggestive of this proposition. Conclusively establishing the relationship between GSS and leadership emergence by women group members in newly constituted computer-mediated decision-making groups will require experimental studies, which should be a high priority for future researchers interested in leadership in computer-mediated contexts.

The spectacular growth of IT has dramatic and profound implications for leadership by women. Specifically, women today are finding greater opportunities in upper management at Web-related companies than at traditional firms. This chapter attributes this state of affairs to the need for talent, an open culture, and the existence of diversified, mixed gender personal networks instead of the all-male "old boy" networks. IT also holds promise as an enabler of leadership emergence by women in middle management decision-making groups.

The accessibility of information has the potential for the development of expert and referent power through information sharing. Moreover, the trend toward the decentralization of decision-making, made possible by the accessibility of information by middle managers, empowers these middle managers of both genders, thus providing women the opportunity to exercise leadership. Finally, computer-mediated communication, such as GSS with its anonymity feature, allows women to increase their participation in decision-making within groups and to emerge as leaders in these groups.

Leadership, defined by Shaw as "an influence process which is directed toward goal achievement," is essential in today's global, competitive environment, which demands both innovation and reduction of costs. When talented individuals are deprived of leadership roles because of gender, whether in upper or middle management, the attainment of organizational goals is jeopardized.

IT plays a significant role in the survival and growth of organizations by contributing to the cracking of the "glass ceiling" in upper management and the removal of barriers to decision-making participation and to the emergence of leadership by women in middle management.

INNOVATIVE CULTURES AND ORGANIZATIONS

Both students of organizations and managers are today increasingly concerned about the capacity of organizations to adapt to rapidly changing environmental conditions. The rate of change in the technological, economic, political, and sociocultural environments is picking up speed, and organizations are, therefore, finding it more and more important to figure out how to adapt.

Adaptation in turbulent environments requires more than minor adjustments to the present way of doing things. It often requires genuinely innovative ideas-new missions, new goals, new products and services, new ways of getting things done, and even new values and assumptions. Most important, adaptation means the developing of the capacity to manage "perpetual change." Organizations must learn "how to learn" and must become "self-designing".

The difficulty is that organizations are by their nature and often by design oriented toward stabilizing and routinizing work. Organizations create cultures that are expressed in structures and processes that permit large numbers of people to coordinate their efforts and that allow new generations of members to continue to perform effectively without having to reinvent the organization each time. How then, can one conceptualize an organization that can function effectively and yet be capable of learning so that it can adapt and innovate in response to changing environmental circumstances?

How can one conceive of an organization that can surmount its own central dynamic that can manage the paradox of institutionalizing and stabilizing the process of change and innovation? In this chapter I want to address some aspects of these questions and to present a point of view based on my research into the dynamics of organizational culture. In particular I want to focus on innovation as being itself a property of culture. In other words, what kind of organizational culture consistently favors innovation?

This question is of special interest at the present time because of the rapid advances being made in the field of information technology (IT). There is ample evidence to suggest that the introduction of IT into organizations not only forces cultural assumptions out into the open but that the potential of IT as a strategic aid to organizations will not be fulfilled unless, at the same time, those organizations develop (or already possess) what I define as innovative cultures.

The definition of innovation is itself a major problem. Defining what is "new" is, of course, also problematic. In analyzing a case of culture change in a large corporation, I found that some of the major changes that the organization felt it had made really reflected an affirmation of some of its most basic assumptions. What, then, had changed? Was there any innovation? My sense about this issue is that we must define innovation ultimately by the perceptions of both members of the organization and those outsiders who interact with the organization and, therefore, who are in a position to perceive changes. If both insiders and informed outsiders agree that something is really "new," then we are dealing with an innovation.

This definition will not satisfy the positivistic empiricist, however. Measuring consensus in perceptions is difficult and messy. But if we are to understand what really goes on in this organizational domain and if we are to arrive at better concepts and theoretical insights, at this stage we will be better off with the rich and messy insights of the ethnographer and the clinician.

In order to lay out these ideas efficiently, the minimal references to what is a vast literature on organization design and innovation had been made. That is, my goal is not to summarize what we know but to be provocative and push into an area of cultural analysis that has not, to my knowledge, been much explored as yet. There are many models available for analyzing organizational systems. Many of them are flawed from the outset, however, because they conceptually separate the task and technical elements from the human and organizational elements.

For example, most models of strategy and organization design advocate that one should start with a concept of mission or goal and then design the organization to fulfill that mission or goal. The human elements are typically thought of as something that follows and must be adapted to the mission and the technical/structural elements. In contrast, a sociotechnical model would indicate that one must integrate the human considerations with the technical ones in the initial design process.

The formulation of the organization's mission and goals is, after all, a product of human beings in entrepreneurial, technical, and managerial roles. The assumptions, beliefs, values, and biases of these human actors thus will limit and bias the technical and structural options considered, and they will certainly affect the organizational design. Furthermore, if the people who will be using a given system (however it may have been invented) do not participate in its design, all kinds of unanticipated problems may arise that will make the system less effective than its technical designers bad forecast. We see this especially in the realm of information technology in which the difficulties of implementation far outstrip the difficulties of invention.

For example, when an information system is designed, the human consequences are often either totally misunderstood or actively ignored. First a "small" example observed by Lotte Bailyn, in which the introduction of PCs to an executive group was slowed down by the frequently discovered fact that most executives cannot type and are not willing to learn to do so. The enthusiastic implementers had created a typing program to deal with this issue and, to provide effective feedback to the learners, arranged to have a bell ring every time a mistake was made (on the theory that an aural signal would get better attention than a visual signal would). But the signal was also public and no one wanted others to know when he or she was making errors, and so the system had to be redesigned with a less vivid but more private feedback signal.

A "larger" example occurred in one division of an aerospace company. The general manager needed detailed performance and schedule information for each project and program in the company and thus designed a system that would provide such detail. The system allowed him to identify schedule or performance problems as soon as they arose, so that he could check on what was going wrong. He felt he needed that information to deal with his outside stakeholders.

What this manager did not anticipate was that the project managers and engineers would feel threatened by the knowledge that their day-to-day behaviour was being monitored. If the manager asked questions about problem areas, they found it difficult to respond because they had not had a chance to look at the reasons for the observed deviations from the established plan.

The system designers should have expected this problem inasmuch as it is a well-known phenomenon in the psychology of control. What typically happens is that subordinates who feel threatened or embarrassed by revealed information attempt to subvert the system by refusing to enter data or by feeding in false information to protect them. Such behaviour usually leads the system designers to invent more elaborate information devices that cannot be falsified, leading to an escalation of resentment and tension in the organization. An even more dangerous outcome is that the subordinates become dependent on the boss to be the control system and cease to exercise whatever self-control they had once had. They might feel that if the President has all the information, let's fix only those problems that he shows himself to be concerned about.

The sociotechnical solution is to involve all the people concerned with the system design. This was eventually done in the preceding case because the manager realized that creating resentment in his subordinates was counterproductive. The whole organization launched into a "redesign" of the system and invented a solution. It concluded that the manager had a valid need for the information but that he did not need it at the same time as all of the employees did. So the project members suggested a time delay; they would get the information as soon as it was available so that they could get to work on any problems that were identified.

The manager would get the same information a couple of days later so that by the time he inquired about problems, or even before he inquired, the project teams could tell him what was wrong and how they were dealing with it. The time delay solved everyone's problems and led to a much more effective organization. The essential control stayed where the information was-in the project teams. Enough is known today about the human problems of information and control systems, about the design of equipment, and about the human problems of automation to make sociotechnical design entirely feasible.

What usually stands in the way is cultural assumptions about the role of management and the role of technical designers in the initial creation of innovations. It is for these reasons that organizational culture must be analyzed first when defining the conditions for adaptation and innovation. This model emphasizes that one can study adaptation and innovation from the point of view of the organizational processes that must be included, from the point of view of the organizational structure that must be in place, and from the point of view of the information technology that must be available.

However, inasmuch as the culture will determine how the technology is ultimately used and will influence both the structure and the processes that the organization uses, it is the cultural assumptions underlying innovation that will influence each of the other elements. Adopting a sociotechnical model reminds us that we cannot bypass the analysis of the cultural and human forces at work in organizations.

The overarching determinant of how organizations work is the culture that evolves in the organization as its members cope with the external problems of survival in the environment and their internal problems of integration. Culture can be defined as the pattern of learned basic assumptions that has worked well enough to be considered valid and, therefore, to be taught to new members as the correct way to perceive, think, and feel in relation to the problems of survival and integration.

Culture manifests itself in overt behaviors, norms, and espoused values, what can be thought of as the artifacts of the culture. Culture is also expressed in some of the less conscious and operational values that members share. But unless one deci phers the underlying, often implicit and unconscious, pattern of assumptions taken for granted, one has not really analyzed the culture.

A culture and its overt manifestations stabilize the daily life of its members and provide meaning for what they do. Stability and hence predictability is essential to the members of an organization. Without predictability they cannot function and thus cannot avoid the anxiety that accompanies a loss of meaning. Culture, once in place, is therefore an inherently conservative force.

The "strength" of a culture is a function of several variables: (1) the strengths of the initial convictions of the organizational founders, (2) the stability of the group or organization, (3) the intensity of the learning experience in terms of the number of crises survived and the emotional intensity of those shared crises, and (4) the degree to which the learning process has been one of anxiety avoidance rather than positive reinforcement. The more the culture helps reduce anxiety, the more it will resist change.

Cultural assumptions tend toward a consistent paradigm to the extent that the culture's creators work from a consistent set of assumptions in the first place and to the extent that the organization's learning experiences provide consistence. If the members of an organization learn inconsistent things in order to survive and remain integrated, they will have inconsistent and possibly ambiguous assumptions with which they nevertheless feel comfortable.

To the extent that culture is a learned product of group experience, there will be a culture wherever there is a group, in the sense of a set of people who share common experiences over a period of time. Inasmuch as most organizations are differentiated over time into many subgroups, there will be subgroup cultures in each of them, with their strengths varying as a function of the aforementioned factors. A total organization, then, can have a total culture as well as a set of subcultures, and any given member of the organization can simultaneously "possess" elements of all of the cultures of which he or she is a member. Some of these will, of course, be family, community, occupational, and other groups that the person belongs to and identifies with outside the organization.

Given that members of organizations have multiple group memberships and that they will identify to different degrees with these various groups, it is not at all anomalous to have a strong overall culture that contains "deviant" elements, or to have entire subcultures that are deviant or countercultural because of their external connections, such as to a strong professional group or an international union.

We know that cultures evolve and can be changed, but we have not analyzed carefully enough the characteristics of any given culture that would more or less facilitate change and innovation. Or, more directly, is it possible to conceive of a type of culture that would be innovative, that would have as its learning dynamic the invention of environmentally responsive new solutions rather than conservative selfpreservation? And is it possible to conceive of a type of culture that would favor sociotechnical design innovations instead of those based on traditional technology?

Cultures are built around and respond to the core technologies that caused the organization to be created in the first place. One may expect organizational cultures to vary, therefore, according to the kind of core technology that is involved. Chemical, hightech, heavy manufacturing, financial, and other service industries each will produce somewhat different "industry" cultures that will influence organizational cultures.All organizations have in common the need to communicate, to get information to the right place at the right time in order to divide labour appropriately and coordinate the effort of the organization's members.

The flow of information can be likened to the lifeblood of the system, and the information channels can be compared with the circulatory system. The state of IT in use at any given time is, therefore, likely to be an important determinant of the organization's capacity to learn. What, then, should be the characteristics of the information system to maximize the capacity of the organization to learn, adapt, and innovate Information technology is central to this analysis because its own evolution has enabled innovative leaps of extraordinary magnitude. Today some organizations are being designed on totally different premises by taking advantage of the IT's capabilities. We can conceptualize this best by distinguishing three kinds of utopian visions that have grown up around IT:

1. The vision to automate: Most of the critical functions in the organization are taken over by robots or computerized systems run by highly skilled and trained professional operators.
2. The vision to "informate": By building accurate models of critical processes in the organization, it is possible not only to automate such processes but also to make the processes themselves visible and understandable to everyone in the organization. This is what Zuboff calls "informating" the organization, and it obviously has tremendous implications for both workers and managers at all levels.

3. Informating up: IT is used to aggregate and centralize as much information as possible about all the parts of the organization, in order to facilitate planning and control by top management. The organization becomes familiar to its top management.
4. Informating down: The design of systems forces an analysis of the core production and other processes of the organization and makes them recognizable to the workers. Instead of understanding only a small piece of the total process, workers become familiar with the whole process and can thus make decisions that previously were made by various layers of management.
5. The vision to transform: A few organizations think of even more radical innovations by asking how one might organize the basic work, the communication patterns, and authority relations, to take advantage of the possibilities inherent in IT. Sociotechnical design considerations become primary in integrating the technical and human capabilities.

Such organizations may take a totally different form, being more like complex networks in which communication and authority chains shift around and change according to the requirements of the task and the motivation and skills of the people. Adaptation and innovation are involved to varying degrees in each of these visions, but in the vision to automate and the vision to informate up, we are talking only of converting existing processes in order to be more efficient.

Thus robots and various other kinds of machine-controlled work are important innovations in the pro duction process, and sophisticated information systems that permit high levels of centralized control are innovations in the degree to which information can be rapidly collected and centralized, but it is only with informating down and transforming that we can get more radical innovation in the nature of the organization itself. In these instances, IT creates new concept of how work is to be done and how the management process itself is to be defined.

What this means is that the cultural assumptions about the nature and use of IT will themselves be crucial determinants of how IT will be used to create further innovation.

ORGANIZATIONAL PROCESSES

Over time, every organization develops a set of processes, recurrent events that ensure that the principal task of the organization is fulfilled and that permit the members of the organization to coordinate effectively with one another. Such processes concern how members communicate with one another, how they solve problems and make decisions, how they implement decisions arrived at, and how they organize work, supervise, reward, punish, and, in general, deal with people.

Such processes reflect the culture as we defined it, but the basic cultural assumptions are largely implicit and invisible, whereas the processes that evolve over time are visible and can be analyzed. In order to understand any given organization, therefore, we need to specify both the underlying assumptions and the observable processes. In our analysis, then, the question is what kinds of cultural assumptions must be present to facilitate organizational processes that will increase the likelihood that the organization will be able to learn, adapt, and innovate?

ORGANIZATIONAL STRUCTURE

Some processes become stable and are articulated in rules, manuals, organization charts, and other more permanent documents reflecting how management feels that things should be done. The ultimate division of labour is embodied in job descriptions and organizational units and is the basic organization design in terms of who reports to whom and who is accountable for what, which is typically thought of as the "formal" structure. But as in the case of organizational processes, this structure really reflects the underlying cultural assumptions.

One of the common misconceptions in this area is that structure can be analyzed as a factor separate from culture. If one starts with a sociotechnical model of organizations, one cannot separate structure from culture. One can, however, ask whether some formal structures are more likely to facilitate or encourage learning, adaptation, and innovation, and if so, what kinds of cultural assumptions will favor the evolution of such structures. In most organizations one also finds an "informal" structure, those processes that are observed to be relatively stable but are supported only by implicit norms and are often regarded to be unsanctioned or even to contradict the formal structure. It is the existence of such counterstruc-tures based on subcultures, or countercultures that may determine what kind of innovation is possible.

The informal structure also includes "compensatory" or "parallel" structures that are designed to offset or supplement what may be weaknesses and dysfunctional elements in the formal structure. Such compensatory or parallel structures may be relatively permanent, such as standing committees, or they may be temporary processes, such as task forces and project teams formed to work only on specific and time-bound tasks. Most organization theories acknowledge that without the informal organization, things simply would not be done effectively, and so the informal structure must be analyzed and understood if we are to comprehend the total system and how it works.

In this chapter the question then becomes what kinds of cultural assumptions would favor the evolution of formal and informal structures that would be likely to lead to learning, adaptation, and innovation? To sum up, I believe that in order to determine the necessary and sufficient conditions for an innovative organization, we must specify those cultural characteristics that favor the kinds of information technology, organizational processes, and formal and informal organizational structures that will increase the likelihood of such innovation.

ORGANIZATION-ENVIRONMENT RELATIONSHIPS

Hypothesis C1: The capacity of an organization to innovate increases to the extent that it assumes that its environments can be controlled, changed, and managed.

Organizations can be distinguished by their shared assumptions regarding the degree to which they dominate or are dominated by their various environments. At one extreme we have organizations that seem completely dependent and assume that their existence and survival is out of their control. They act fatalistic and are passive in the face of environmental turbulence. They accept whatever niche the environment provides.

At the other extreme are organizations that share the assumption that their own behaviour will influence the environment and that their survival and growth depend on the extent to which they can dominate some aspects of their environment. Also implied is the assumption that progress and improvement are possible, a basically optimistic orientation toward the environment.

Innovative capacity increases to the extent that members assume that innovation is possible and necessary, which derives from their optimistic assumption that the environment can be influenced. Organizations that pessimistically assume that they are dominated by others and/or that their environments are fixed find it difficult to conceive of new ideas and find it even more difficult to marshal the energy to try them out.

THE NATURE OF HUMAN ACTIVITY

Hypothesis C2: The capacity of an organization to innovate increases to the extent that it assumes that the appropriate human activity is to be proactive, to be oriented toward problem solving, and to improve things.

All organizations make implicit assumptions about whether the appropriate behaviour of their members is to be (1) reactive, fatalistic, and oriented to getting what pleasure one can out of one's lot in life (Dionysian); (2) to be proactive, optimistic, and oriented toward improving things (Promethean); or (3) to take the middle ground of trying to harmonize and compromise between one's own needs and whatever environmental constraints and possibilities exist

(Apollonian). These assumptions are the individual-level counterpart to the assumptions relating the organization to its environment.

An innovator in the midst of reactive or harmonizing people will find it virtually impossible to get even an audience, much less a commitment to new ways of doing things. In Dionysian or Apollonian organizations, innovators are likely to be called whistle-blowers, boat rockers, or troublemakers and thus to be neutralized. And if the culture is too fatalistic, it will not, of course, attract or retain innovators in the first place.

One may wish to speculate whether there is an upper limit to activity orientation. If there are too many innovators and if the culture strongly encourages innovation, will that cause other problems that, in the end, will undermine innovation by making life too chaotic and unpredictable? I believe not, because if too much innovation becomes a problem, the organization will invent processes and structures that reduce innovation to a tolerable level. In other words, if the organization is going out of control, its own innovativeness will enable it to invent mechanisms to achieve greater discipline and control. The reverse is not true, however. An organization that is too passive or fatalistic cannot invent "proactivity." It will stagnate until it fails or is taken over by others who will forcibly change the culture by replacing its employees with people oriented toward a different activity. I am hypothesizing, therefore, that one cannot have too much innovativeness but that one can have too much conservatism and passivity.

THE NATURE OF REALITY AND TRUTH

Hypothesis C3: The capacity of an organization to innovate increases to the extent that it assumes that truth is to be arrived at by pragmatic (vs. moralistic) means.

Organizations can be distinguished by the degree to which they share assumptions about how one determines whether or not something is true. When a complex decision has to be made regarding uncertain futures and information of uncertain validity, what criteria does the organization use to determine when it has enough and the right kind of information to make the decision?

At one extreme one finds a heavy reliance on tradition, dogma, the authority of moral principles, or the wisdom of elders. At the other extreme one finds pragmatism embodied in either a search for scientific verification or a trial- and error-attitude if formal verification is not possible or practical. If the decision is in a domain in which verification by physical means is not possible, pragmatism would imply that the decision makers debate the issues and subject each alternative to sufficient scrutiny that the one that survives can be accepted with some measure of confidence.

In organizations dominated by dogma or authorities of various sorts, it is not only difficult to articulate new ideas but even more difficult to obtain permission to try them out. An exception is, of course, the situation in which the innovator is the person in authority, a situation that arises from time to time in history but that is hard to specify as an organizational condition or to predict. To increase the innovative capacity generally, a positive value must be put on novelty, on breaking tradition, and on trying out new things even if they are risky, and such a value must be supported by an underlying assumption that "the truth" is not already known.

The pragmatic end of the continuum also implies a more positive attitude toward trial and error, risk taking, and the acceptance of unsuccessful efforts or failures. The more committed the organization is to dogmas, rules, systems, and procedures that become institutionalized; the harder it will be for its members to take the risks necessary for innovation to succeed. The message in such moralistic organizations is "try new things only if you are sure you will not break rules or fail," which is surely a prescription for conservatism and playing it safe.

THE NATURE OF TIME

Hypothesis C4A: The capacity of an organization to innovate increases to the extent that it is oriented to the near future (vs. past, present, or far future). Hypothesis C4B: The capacity of an organization to innovate increases to the extent that it uses medium-length time units (vs. short ones that do not allow innovation to develop or long ones that make innovation difficult to evaluate).

All organizations hold implicit assumptions about the relative importance of the past, the present, and the future, and all organizations have implicit assumptions about the appropriate length of time units for different kinds of tasks. Some organizations measure themselves in short units such as weeks or months; others use intermediate units such as quarters and years; and still others use longer units such as five or 10 years. All organizations use all of these units for various different purposes, and as Lawrence and Lorsch pointed out years ago, the different functional units of an organization such as sales and research and development have different assumptions about what it means to be "on time" and how long the units of work are.

It is likely that in each organization's culture, there are assumptions about the "really important" time units. The actual size of the relevant time units varies from company to company, so what is "past," "present," "near future," and "far future" must be determined for each organization, by getting the members' consensus on these units. The size of such time units is also influenced by the core technologies with which the organization is working. The development of new products, for example, takes much longer in the pharmaceutical industry than in the consumer goods industry.

Organizations that live in the past or present find it difficult to place a value on novelty, because they are focusing on what has worked or is working now. People with new ideas can be dismissed easily because their ideas do not "fit" what the organization likes to think about. On the other hand, if the organization is concentrating on the far future, it may not be able to launch any innovations because it assumes that there is always plenty of time to try things "in the future." A near-future orientation should, therefore, be most favorable to innovation. It is also clear that too short a time orientation always makes innovation difficult because one can always show that short-run costs are too high to justify continuing the trial and error necessary for innovation. On the other hand, if the time units are too long, some innovations that fail will be allowed to continue too long; the organization will lose money; and the whole innovation process will be undermined because people will remember how they were hurt by past innovations. The organization's ability to decide on an optimal length of time for an innovation thus becomes an important determinant of its learning capacity.

This optimal length of time is subjectively defined in most organizations and must be measured within each organization. The precise length of the units is not as important as the members' ability to recognize that giving an innovation too little or too much time is equally destructive to the overall innovation process. Optimal-length time units also play a role in selling an innovative vision, whether that comes from leaders or from other innovators in the organization. The vision of the future cannot exceed the ability of the organization's members to understand what is proposed, nor can it promise benefits that will be realized only by the next generation. To be motivated to implement something new, people have to be able to see the benefits that it will bring them within their own lifetime.

As Jaques argued, the length of time over which organization members have "discretion" appears to vary with organizational rank. On the shop floor, supervisors check on employees by the hour or the day. At lower managerial levels, one has discretion over weeks, and so on up the ladder until the most senior management is supposed to define its tasks in terms of years. In communicating the future impact of proposed innovations, it becomes critical, then, to consider over what time units the audience is used to thinking. "Optimal" time units, in this context, are partly defined by the actual innovative task that is being proposed or undertaken.

THE NATURE OF HUMAN NATURE

Hypothesis C5: The capacity of an organization to innovate increases to the extent that it assumes that people are ultimately neutral or good and, in any case, is capable of improvement.

Organizations make implicit assumptions about human nature, both whether it is good, neutral, or evil and how malleable or fixed it is. If organizations are cynical about human nature, they will not encourage innovation or, worse, will suspect innovators of having ulterior motives. In such organizations, innovative capacity often is devoted to defeating organizational goals. Workers invent elaborate processes and devices to make life easier for themselves at the expense of organizational efficiency.

On the other hand, if the organization holds optimistic assumptions about human nature, it will expect people to be innovative, will encourage innovation, will listen to new ideas, and will be more likely to trust them. At the same time, for innovation to be encouraged, the organization's members must feel that they all are "perfectible" in the sense that their personality and contribution are not fixed. If one knows one can grow and improve, this knowledge (assumption) can act as a powerful stimulant to personal development and innovation.

THE NATURE OF HUMAN RELATIONSHIPS

Hypothesis C6A: The capacity of an organization to innovate increases to the extent that it assumes the ideal of individualism and the pursuit of individual diversity.

Hypothesis C6B: But if an organization has a few innovative individuals whose ideas are adopted, it can implement some types of innovation faster, to the extent that it assumes the ideal of groupism.

Hypothesis C6C: The capacity of an organization to innovate increases to the extent that it assumes that collegial or participative methods of decision making are the most appropriate.

Hypothesis C6D: But if an organization has innovative people in senior leadership roles, it can implement some innovations faster, to the extent that it assumes authoritarian or paternalistic methods of decision making.This dimension of culture pertains to prevailing assumptions about the ideal human relationship. Two dimensions are involved here:

1. The degree to which the organization assumes the ideal of "individualism" (that all good things come from individual effort) or "groupism" (that all good things come from the group, implying that all individuals must subordinate themselves to the group).
2. The degree to which ideal relationships are seen as collegial or participative (implying that power and influence in decision making depends on who has what expertise relevant to any given task to be accomplished) or as autocratic or paternalistic (implying that power and influence reside in positions, statuses, and roles or are a function of the individual's specific personality).

The hypotheses regarding these two dimensions are more complex and contingent because under certain conditions innovation can occur anywhere along them. Generally, a culture that values individuals and individual diversity has more ideas from which to draw and creates more incentives for ideas to be put forward. However, when it comes to accepting ideas and implementing them, the strongly individualistic organization may be at some disadvantage. In other words, in a groupist organization it is harder to get new ideas to be articulated, but if they are adopted, such an organization will be far more effective in implementing them because any individuals who may dissent will suppress their dissent for the sake of the group's welfare.

In such organizations the burden of innovation probably falls on the leaders, in that they are the most likely to be able to get an idea adopted in the first place. What the determinants are of innovativeness in the leaders of groupist organizations then becomes the secondary, but critical, question. Collegial or participative decision making is more likely to identify the relevant areas in which innovation is needed, to advance good ideas, to stimulate creativity, and to produce a state of affairs in which everyone understands the idea so that it can be properly implemented. This assumption is central because collegial or participative decision making influences so many phases of the total innovation process, from invention to implementation, particularly if the new idea or process is complex and hard to understand. If, on the other hand, an autocratic or paternalistic leader has innovative ideas that are sound, if the ideas are not too complex to communicate, and if the sociotechnical implications have been correctly thought through, it will be possible for the or ganization to implement such ideas more rapidly and more completely.

The danger in this situation, however, is threefold: (1) that the leader will impose an idea that is wrong and the subordinates are neither motivated nor rewarded for pointing out the potential problems; (2) that the idea will not be successfully communicated, leading to paralysis and frustration; or (3) that the idea will be implemented incorrectly because the leader did not discover that the subordinates did not fully understand what he or she had in mind and/or did not accept the consequences of the innovation.

One additional point bearing on this assumption needs to be discussed: If predictions about the ultimate impact of IT are correct, then leaner, flatter, and more highly networked organizations are the likely consequence. Such organizations cannot work effectively, however, if their managers are still operating from hierarchical models buttressed by autocratic or paternalistic assumptions. The basis of authority in such networks is more likely to be the degree of skill or expertise that any given member has at any given moment in time, relative to the task to be done. Positional authority will mean very little. Obviously such systems will function better if they hold collegial or participative assumptions in the first place.

SUBCULTURAL DIVERSITY

Hypothesis C7: The capacity of an organization to innovate increases to the extent that it encourages diverse but connected subcultures.

As organizations grow and mature, they develop subcultures as well as overarching cultures. The nature and diversity of such subcultures influence the organization's innovative capacity. For any given group, culture is a homogenizing force. However, if the organization contains in its total system enough diverse subsystems with their own diverse subcultures, it can innovate by empowering people and ideas from those subcultures that are most different from the "parent" yet are best adapted to a changing environment. Drawing on diverse subcultures is, in fact, the most common way that cultures evolve, and this process, if properly managed, is therefore one of the most important sources of innovation.

Such subcultures must be connected and part of a parent culture or their elements will not be seen as relevant if introduced into the parent. For example, in a highly geographically decentralized organization, new ideas may well spring up in an overseas subsidiary, but these ideas can be imported by the parent organization only if the subsidiary is perceived to be part of the larger culture. If the ideas are brought in by transferring people from the subsidiary, those people will have credibility and influence only if they are perceived to be part of the larger culture and sympathetic to it.

It is this diversity-within-unity theme that accounts for so many current management statements that the effective organization is one that can both centralize and decentralize, that can be loose and tight at the same time. To restate the point, diversification and decentralization are effective as innovative forces only if the separate units are perceived to be, and feel them to be, connected to the whole. Conversely, if they do not feel connected, they will not be motivated to innovate on behalf of the whole. If they are not perceived to be connected, their ideas will not be perceived as relevant.

5

Focus on Women and Information Technology

Scholars exploring gender and technology interactions have tended to concentrate on gender and technology in the workforce and somewhat less on women as users of technology. Limited studies explored how technological designs, especially for information technologies (IT), might differ depending on the gender of the designer and user. In this chapter I explore some contributions of feminist theories, ranging from liberal feminism through radical feminism to postcolonial feminism, to the understanding of gender and information technology.

Attempt will be here to use the framework provided by the perspective of each feminist theory to examine at least one example from each of the three following areas: women in the information technology workforce, women as users of information technology, and women and information technology design. Since each theory tended to evolve in response to a deficit or exclusionary perspective perceived in previous theories, examining information technology and gender using the fuller range of feminist theories uncovers subtle, rich insights into the dynamics of gender and technology.

The term cyberfeminism, which explicitly fuses gender and information technology, arose in the late 1980s and early

1990s. As Hawthorne and Klein note in their book, *Cyberfeminism*: "Just as there are liberal, socialist, radical and postmodern feminists, so too one finds these positions reflected in the interpretations of cyberfeminism." Because cyberfeminism appears currently to pick and choose among aspects of various feminist theories in a somewhat uncritical fashion without developing a coherent or successor theory, I conclude the chapter with a brief exploration of what each of the feminist theories suggests for this less developed theory of cyberfeminism.

A general definition of liberal feminism is the belief that women are suppressed in contemporary society because they suffer unjust discrimination. Liberal feminists seek no special privileges for women and simply demand that everyone receive equal consideration without discrimination on the basis of sex.

WORKFORCE

When it comes to information technology jobs, most engineers and others involved with information technology take a liberal feminist stance and assume that the focus should be on employment, access, and discrimination issues. Social scientists studying the gender distribution of the technology workforce point out that historically and today, the technology workforce represents a vertically and horizontally gender-stratified labour market, with women concentrated in the lowest-paid positions, closest to the most tedious, hands-on making of the products and furthest from the creative design of technology.

Most women working in the IT industry engage in the tedious, eye-straining work of electronic assembly. Men predominate in the decision-making, creative design sectors as venture capitalists, computer scientists, and engineers producing startups, new software, and hardware design.

DESIGN

Liberal feminists would seek to remove barriers that prevent equal access for women to information technology jobs not only to provide economic equality but to provide access to higher-paying jobs for women. Unequal access has implications that go well beyond the composition of the workforce. Two decades ago, biologists revealed that a predominance of male scientists tended to introduce bias by excluding females as experimental subjects, focusing on problems of primary interest to males, employing faulty experimental designs, and interpreting data based in language or ideas constricted by patriarchal parameters.

This exclusion bias resulted in under-diagnosis, inappropriate treatment, and higher death rates for cardiovascular and other diseases in women. Male dominance in engineering and the creative decision-making sectors of the IT workforce may result in similar bias, particularly design and user bias.

USE

Having large numbers of male engineers and creators of technologies also often results in technologies that are useful from a male perspective (that is, these technologies fail to address important issues for women users). Many studies have explored the overt and covert links between the military, engineering and masculinity, and design and use of technology. For example, Janet Abbate studied the origins of the Internet in ARPANET. The unique improvement of the Internet was that it was a network, overcoming the vulnerability to nuclear attack of the previous star configuration computer network.

Liberal feminism suggests that now that they have become aware of potential bias in design or user-friendliness, both male and female engineers and information technology creators can correct for failures to include women and their needs and interests. By definition, liberal feminism does not address the potential of gender to affect "fundamentals" (that is, do women engineers define, approach, or discover different fundamentals such as string theory?). Since liberal feminism reaffirms rather than challenges positivism and individualism, it suggests that "fundamentals" would always remain the same.

SOCIALIST FEMINISM

In contrast to liberal feminism, socialist feminism rejects individualism and positivism. Marxist critiques form the historical precursors and foundations for socialist feminist critiques and define all knowledge, including science, as socially constructed and emerging from practical human involvement in production. Since knowledge is a productive activity of human beings, it cannot be objective and value-free, because the basic categories of knowledge are shaped by human purposes and values. In the early twenty-first-century United States, capitalism, the prevailing mode of production, determines technology and favors the interests of the dominant class.

This Marxist-socialist theory under-girds the work of numerous scholars of technology who have produced a large body of research commonly known as "the social shaping of technology." This phrase categorizes information technology as a social product and suggests that information technology comprises human activities and "know-how." Feminist scholars rightly point out that technology and the social shaping of technology have often been conceptualized in terms of men, excluding women at all levels. Socialist feminist critiques include women and place gender on equal footing with class in shaping technology.

In this dual-systems approach capitalism and patriarchy function as mutually reinforcing parts of a system where the sexual division of labour stands with wage labour as a central feature of capitalism, and where gender differences in wages, while failing to count women's contributions to reproduction and child rearing as "productivity" in a capitalist economy, reinforce patriarchy and power differentials in the home.

Class and gender analyses document women's occupation of the worst-paid, most tedious and health-destroying segment of the labour market in electronics assembly-etching circuits onto wafers of silicon, dipping circuits into vats of carcinogenic solvents, and peering through microscopes for seven to ten hours a day to bond wires to silicon chips. Socialist feminist analyses reveal that the extremely low wages paid women in these jobs, along with women's geographic immobility, may lead to work done by men, although less menial and more difficult to automate, being automated more quickly in order to keep wages low, to destroy unions, or both.

Socialist feminist approaches also suggest reasons that men dominate the creation of new technologies, since access to venture capital, geographic mobility, and ability to work long hours may be as critical to the success of start-ups as is technological expertise. In 1999, when John Chambers, president and CEO of Cisco Systems, made $121,701,629 in salary and stock options, "real incomes for the poorest 20 per cent of all households in the region fell by 8 per cent, while rising by 2 per cent in California overall."

Understandings of class relations emerging under capitalism and gender relations under patriarchy help to explain the intertwining of military and masculinity that drives the choices made to develop technologies in a certain way and much technological innovation in this country and elsewhere. Current intellectual property rights agreements and laws provide opportunities for choices in technology development that further exacerbate class differences by transferring technologies developed using public moneys to the private realm through patents.

The decisions about which products are developed fall under the influence of capitalist interests in profit margins. Such intellectual property rights function as a form of privatization, permitting decisions of product development to occur in the private, rather than the public, realm. Capitalist interests in the bottom line rather than in public needs and interests dictate which "products" are developed. In the patenting of intellectual property, rights (and profits) are transferred from the public, which paid for the research with its tax dollars, to the private company, start-up dot.com, institution, or individual who controls the patent.

Socialist feminists might view this as a transfer from the pockets of the workers who pay the taxes to underwrite federal research to the patent holders in the private sector who will reap massive profits, and thus see it as serving the interests of bourgeois capitalists. New technologies in computer science and engineering are often developed using federal grants (paid for by taxes).

Understanding that middle- and upper-class men create and design most new information technology and serve as the sources of money for design and creation, explains much about whose needs are met by current technology and its design. Socialist feminist reform suggests that the allocation of resources for technology development should be determined by greatest benefit for the common good. A growing use of cyberprotests to disrupt capitalist enterprises such as the World Bank might be seen by socialists as an example of information technology use for the common good.

Just as socialist feminist theory provided insights into the gender and class distributions of the technology labour market, African American critiques uncover the place or role of race in the distribution. Racism intertwines and reinforces differing aspects of capitalism and patriarchy.

African Americans and Hispanics are underrepresented in engineering and in the upper end of the technology workforce, relative to their percentage in the overall United States population (22.4 percent). In 1998, African Americans constituted 3 percent of engineers and 4 percent of computer and mathematical scientists; 2.5 percent to 3 percent of engineers and of mathematical and computer scientists identified themselves as Hispanic. Although traditionally defined as a career path for mobility from the working to middle-class, engineering is pursued by disproportionately fewer blacks and Latinos than whites; even fewer African American women and Latinas, relative to their male counterparts, become engineers or scientists.

In stark contrast, women of colour are disproportionately represented in the lowest-paying and highest-health-risk portions of the information technology labour force. Women of colour occupy the ghettos in the cities where the electronic assembly occurs.

Like socialist feminism, African American/womanist feminism, based on African American critiques of a Eurocentric approach to knowledge, rejects individualism and positivism for social constructionist approaches and questions methods that distance the observer from the object of study. Because technology involves practical application of more abstract, basic scientific research, the problem of the distance between engineer (researcher) and the technology (object of study) needs to be understood, discussed, and addressed to make technological research methodologies clearer to both developers and users.

Unlike theoretical scientific projects, which do not necessarily have immediate practical outcomes, projects in computer science or engineering must accommodate the impact of the uses of technology with particular attention to the users of technology. When designing technologies, engineers, designers, and computer scientists should not only ask how and under what conditions the technology will be used, but also allow the potential consumer to shape the design of the product. The digital divide that has led to 60 percent of all African Americans and 68 percent of all Hispanics lacking access to the Internet shapes the perception of the potential consumer. Gender, class, and race, along with other factors such as age and ability status should be considered in defining who the user will be.

Along with the importance of having a team representing varied intellectual and technical backgrounds, diversity in gender and race is beginning to be understood as critical to designing complex technologies. Historically, technology reflected and reinforced race relations, and traditional Web programming has typically ignored minorities. For example, initially the Blacksburg Electronic Village, an on-line community network, "routed around" race and relied on the "digital default" of white, male, heterosexual, middle-aged, middle- to upper-class. Socialist feminist and African American feminist theories imply that women computer scientists, through a collective process of political and scientific struggle, might produce technologies different from those produced by men of any race or class.

These technologies might reflect the priorities of more people and be user-accessible and user-friendly for more people because they would be based in the experience of women, whose standpoint as the non-dominant group in IT provides them with a more comprehensive view of reality because of their race, class, and gender. Anita Borg, founder of the Institute for Women and Technology contended that "high-tech firms are missing the boat by having a disproportionately male workforce that is unable or at least unlikely-to dream up a full range of products appealing to women."

EXISTENTIALIST FEMINISM

In contrast to essentialism, which posits biological bases for differences between males and females, existentialist feminism purports that it is not the biological differences themselves but the value society assigns to biological differences between males and females that has led woman to play the role of the Other. The philosophical origins of existentialist feminism emphasize that it is man's conception of woman as Other that has led to his willingness to dominate and exploit her.

The gender stratification of the technology labour market, in which men occupy the higher-paying roles of engineer and designer and women occupy the lower-paying position of worker is a value assignment based on biological differences between the sexes. As Frissen's work demonstrates, women do the casual work of word processing and telecommuting in their homes; this lower-paid work fits with women's role as Other and the value assigned to her role in child care by society.

As Webster points out, "the 'objectivity' which is aspired to in the design process is the viewpoint of the men who design." De Beauvoir described the phenomenon as follows: "Representation of the world, like the world itself, is the work of men; they describe it from their own point of view, which they confuse with the absolute truth."

The computing industry in its language as well as its hardware reflects the world of the designers. That world reflects the world of men who spend less time in child care and have relatively more time to "crack the code."

> And once you've done that [spent hours in front of screens]... you'd know there were things you could exchange, a level of hints and tips, but more deeply a level of understanding, shared language... but they [those men] don't look around and see the absence of women, they don't perhaps think that they are creating a language, and perhaps, as it's expressed at work, a power-base which is exclusive. And they don't realize that they are where they are because the computing industry is designed for them. It's designed for people who have got hours to spare: in the garage, or the shed, or the attic, cracking the code.

Use Videogames overwhelmingly reflect men's interests and the military origins of much of the "gaming" industry with the focus on violence, explosions, and killing. Since males predominate as videogame players and since the object for commercial videogame developers is to make money, videogame developers have demonstrated reluctance to change the successful formulae, known to appeal to men and boys, to produce videogames likely to appeal more to women and girls. This development around the male norm excludes women as users of the technology.

PSYCHOANALYTIC FEMINISM

Dinnerstein and Chodorow have used an aspect of psychoanalytic theory known as object relations theory to examine the construction of gender and sexuality during the Oedipal stage of psychosexual development, which usually results in male dominance. They conclude that the gender differences resulting in male dominance can be traced to the fact that in our society, women are the primary caretakers for most infants and children. Keller in particular applied the work of Chodorow and Dinnerstein to show how science, populated mostly by men, has become a masculine province in its choice of experimental topics; use of male subjects for experimentation, interpretation, and theorizing from data; and the practice and applications of science undertaken by the scientists.

Keller suggests that since the scientific method stresses objectivity, rationality, distance, and autonomy of the observer from the object of study (that is, the positivist neutral observer), individuals who feel comfortable with independence, autonomy, and distance will be more likely to become scientists. This objectivity and rationality of science have become synonymous with a male approach to the physical, natural world. Encouraged to be independent, autonomous, and distant, male engineers and computer scientists design technologies and IT systems reflecting those characteristics.

As Bodker and Greenbaum suggest, the "hard-systems" approach to computer systems developments follow the positivist, linear, and technicist approach compatible with Western scientific thought. The technical capabilities, constraints of the machines, and rational data flow become the focus and driver of the technology design. This hard-systems design approach used by developers (mostly male) of computer systems assumes separation, distance, and independence on at least two levels:

1. Between the abstract systems development and the concrete real world of work. Separation ignores the often circular and interconnected forces of organization, assuming that they remain linear and unaffected by other hierarchical power relations.
2. Between the developers and users. Since users do not contribute to the design of the system, their needs and suggestions that might make the system function more smoothly in the real world of work are ignored. The problems caused by this abstraction, objectivity, autonomy, and separation have spawned new methods to solve the problems and mediate the gap, such as "soft-systems" human factors approaches.

The gender constellation predicted by psychoanalytic feminism becomes transparent: The men design hardware systems in ways that reflect their perspective on the world, which tends to place priority on data and ignore relationships between people. Women, socialized to value connections and relationships, tend to feel uncomfortable with the hard systems approach and as users find that the technology fails to aid much of the real-world work.

The design inhibits or fails to foster good teamwork and other coworker relationships. Because the design does not reflect women's view of priorities in the organization and the work actively ignores the reality of power and gender relations, women tend to be excluded and to exclude themselves from hard-systems design. Psychoanalytic feminist perspective critiques raise the very interesting question of how systems design might change if more feminine values and connection became priorities. Sorenson explored whether male and female computer scientists worked differently and found that men tended to focus on mathematical models and computer programming while women spent more time running experiments, reading scientific literature, and plotting data, leading to "caring values" of empathy and rationale of responsibility.

After studying the technological and political values of men and women engineering students, graduate students, and junior R & D scientists at the Norwegian Institute of Technology, Sorenson concluded, "In computer science, this means that women have a caring, other-oriented relationship to nature and to people, an integrated, more holistic and less hierarchical world-view, a less competitive way of relating to colleagues and a greater affinity to users."

Understanding the importance of relationships and power, some women computer scientist designers have attempted to link users with systems design as an explicit attempt to empower women. Some might view this as an example of Harding's "strong objectivity," in which starting from marginalized lives adds perspectives to reveal

Eurocentric and androcentric elements in the framework of traditional positivist objectivity, thereby strengthening it. This shortening of distance between the user and the system design also mimics Keller's description of less autonomy, independence, and separation as classic hallmarks of psychoanalytic feminism for McClintock's work in A Feeling for the Organism.

RADICAL FEMINISM

Radical feminism maintains that women's oppression is the first, most widespread, and deepest oppression. Scientific institutions, practice, and knowledge are particularly male-dominated and have been documented by many feminists to be especially effective patriarchal tools for controlling and harming women. Radical feminism rejects most scientific theories, data, and experiments not only because they exclude women but also because they are not women-centered.

Some might define the work of Bratteteig and her coworkers as radical feminism, because it originates from women's discourse on computer science problems and methods. Indeed, they insist on prioritizing applicability of systems and putting users and developers in the same plane as collaborators in systems development. This focus on women, starting from the understanding of a woman worker and her abilities and then centering on how her professional competence can be augmented by the use of a system, does begin with women's experience and is consistent with feminist principles.

MacKinnon suggests that the consciousness-raising group provides a methodology for radical feminism in addition to the focus on women and the empowerment of women. Because patriarchy pervades and dominates all institutions, ideologies, and technologies, women have difficulty placing their experiences, lives, and needs in central focus in their everyday lives and environments. Using their personal experiences as a basis, women meet in communal, nonhierarchical consciousness-raising groups to examine their experiences to determine what counts as knowledge.

In her work at Xerox Palo Alto Research Center (PARC), Lucy Suchman uses this approach in her view that knowledge held by users is central to the design process. They are "taking computerization as an occasion to articulate unacknowledged forms of expertise and to take that knowledge seriously as a basis for design." In recognizing the gap between technologies created by experts and their use in real working environments, they have produced a "radical reconceptualisation of the computer systems development process which recognizes the innovatory character of the implementation process and places the local expertise of users at the centre."

The interplay between designing and use, or designer and user, described in the Suchman example also might be seen to demonstrate the cyclicity often associated with radical feminism. Cyclicity as a conception of time and thinking as an upward spiral seem more appropriate ways to study a world where everything is connected in a process of constant change.

Radical feminists might interpret the binary 0,1 foundation of computers and computing as based upon the primary male-female dichotomy and dualism. The "switchers," "controls," and "operations" language of computing fit the patriarchal mode of control. The dichotomy receives reinforcement by the dominance of men and relative absence of women from the design process. "So, the domination of men and the absence of women from the design process is one factor which creates technologies which are closely geared to the needs of men and which are inappropriate to women's requirements."

Radical feminism suggests that because men, masculinity, and patriarchy have become completely intertwined with technology and computer systems in our society, no truly feminist alternative to technology exists. Although various groups have used cyberactivism to protest political military action, imagining technology from a woman-centered perspective in the absence of patriarchy becomes extremely difficult, if not impossible. Since engineering and technology development in the Western and Northern hemispheres emphasize control-control over nature, over people, and over machines-imagining a technology premised on cooperation, collaboration, and working with nature, people, and machines runs contrary to our image of the technology that evolved in a patriarchal, heterosexist society.

Although often considered an outgrowth of radical feminism, queer and transgender theories actually question links between sex, gender, and sexual orientation. They raise additional challenges about the links between economic, racial, and dominance factors and gender in our society. As Judith Butler argues, the very act of defining a gender identity excludes or devalues some bodies and practices, while simultaneously obscuring the constructed character of gender identity; describing gender identity creates a norm. The creators of The Turing Game, a computer game modification of Alan Turing's suggestion of ways to differentiate machines from people and men from women, explain their goals and methodologies in the following terms:

> Do men and women behave differently online? Can you tell who is a man and who is a woman based on how they communicate and interact with others on the Internet? Can you tell how old someone is, or determine their race or national origin? In the online world as in the real world, these issues of personal identity affect how we relate to others. Societies are created and destroyed by these understandings and misunderstandings in the real world. Yet, as the online world becomes increasingly a part of our lives, identity in this new medium is still poorly understood. At the Georgia Institute of Technology, we have created an online game to help us explore and teach about these issues.
>
> This environment, called The Turing Game, is a game of identity deception, expression, and discovery. Available on the Internet, it has been played by more than 9000 people. Players from seventy-six countries on all seven continents have used the game to learn about issues of identity and diversity online through direct experience. At the same time, they have created communities of their own, and explored

the boundaries of electronic communication. The game explores the creations of these norms and how the Internet opens possibilities for identity changes and deception.

POSTMODERN FEMINISM

In postmodernism, the self is no longer regarded as "masterful, universal, integrated, autonomous, and self-constructed; rather it is socially constructed by ideology, discourse, the structure of the unconscious, and/or language." In contrast to liberal feminism, postmodernism dissolves the universal subject and postmodern feminism dissolves the possibility that women speak in a unified voice or that they can be universally addressed. Postmodern perspectives stress that due to her situatedness-the result of her specific national, class, and cultural identities-the category of woman can no longer be regarded as smooth, uniform, and homogeneous.

Postmodern feminist theories imply that no universal research agenda or application of technologies will be appropriate and that various women will have different reactions to technologies depending upon their own class, race, sexuality, country, and other factors. This definition of postmodern feminism parallels the description of the complex and diverse coevolution of women and computing.

As postmodern feminist theory recognizes limitations with perceiving women as a universal group, so have deeper, more complex studies of technology industries revealed limitations of simplistic assumptions in technology designs. For example, Webster suggests that critiquing the absence of understanding of women's needs is easier than identifying what women's needs and priorities really are.

First of all, they are of course not uniform across all women or across all social classes, nationalities and cultures. Then, making the link between women's needs and the consequently desirable features of an IT system is a vexed question, and one that is too often dealt with in an essentialist manner by reference to the supposedly universal characteristics of women IT users (for example, as lacking in confidence with computers, as disinterested in computers except as tools, as caring and sociable rather than rational and technical).

Feminist design initiatives have often encountered this difficulty. Most have addressed it by focusing away from the eventual characteristics of the IT products which they shape, and towards the processes of shaping which offer scope for permanently redefining the role of female users in systems design.

Workforce Just as women's needs for IT or technology designs differ and vary, industrial employment of women also does not fit a universal or uniform pattern. Innovations in technology have not led to overall restructuring of established sexual divisions of labour, or unequal gender or race relations. Some groups of women have improved or lost ground in their employment in technology industries. For example, some women have benefited from programs designed to increase female representation in IT and other technology industries. These equity and access programs (based in liberal feminist theories) have benefited some professional middle-class women whose educational backgrounds position them to capitalize on better employment opportunities.

Although relocation and temporization of work have tended to hurt employees in general and women in particular, the effects may depend upon urban location. For example, closing offices in city centers and metropolitan areas has tended to hurt urban women, who are more likely to be of lower socioeconomic status and of colour, while creating employment for women in the suburbs. In contrast, development of offshore information processing has improved employment for women in poorer countries. Information and data processing functions, once performed by women in the First World have now been exported to low-cost economies because telecommunications and satellite technologies make this possible.

Similarly, the "flexibility" and "casualization" of the workforce that telecommuting permits may hurt wages, benefits and long-term stability. Although it creates or increases the double burden for women who can mind children while working at home, some women prefer this option to no work at all. But ICTs can also directly allow women to handle paid and unpaid work simultaneously. A simple example is the cell phone. Frissen suggests that it allows working women to transform the double burden of home and work into a parallel burden, allowing them to multitask and manage their domestic responsibilities better (from a distance).

This remark suggests why different women may react differently to technologies, depending upon their race, class, age, ability status, parental status, urban-rural location, or other factors. Coupled with the rapid and changing pace of technology, postmodern feminism suggests why universal theories fail to fit the reality of women's lives. The lack of universalism may inhibit gender-based coalitions and organizing, making it easier to understand the political inactivism of which individuals who articulates postmodern perspectives may be accused.

POSTCOLONIAL FEMINISM

The acquisition of territories by European nations that peaked during the late nineteenth century is defined as colonialism, i.e., the conquest and direct control of other people's land, and often is described as a particular phase in the history of imperialism or the globalization of the capitalist mode of production. Accumulation of and control over knowledge of science, history, geography, language, literature, art, and anthropology of the colonized people or the Other accompanied the control of the land.

Although the wave marking the end of colonial rule beginning in 1947, following various campaigns of anticolonial resistance, created high hope for a proper postcolonial era, the extent to which the West had maintained control became clear quickly. The continuing Western influence, particularly in the economic arena but also in the political, ideological, and military sectors, became known as neocolonialism by Marxists. Feminists have suggested that patriarchy dominates postcolonial and neocolonial life, much as it dominated everyday colonial life.

The term postcolonial remains problematic for many, since the United States and other Western countries continue to intervene militarily, especially in the Middle East and Africa, and certainly exert considerable control over the economy and knowledge production of most formerly colonized countries. Postcolonial discourse, culture, and knowledge production in developing countries also exhibit substantial ties to the imperialist country, and a major project of the postcolonial critiques focuses on decentering the relationship of the former peripheral colony to the former central imperialist country.

Not surprisingly, technologies reflect the varying complex aspects of the interrelationships among developed and developing countries in general and between the particular cultures of the colonized and colonizing country. General themes include the underdevelopment of the southern continents by Europe and other northern continents; the idea that the culture, science, and technology of the colonizer or former colonizing country remains superior to that of the colony or postcolonial country; and the insistence that developing countries must restructure their local economies to become scientifically and technologically literate enough to join and compete in a global economy.

In northern former colonizing countries, the concurrent restructuring effects of multinational corporations and other forces of globalization are evidenced in downsizing, privatization, and widening economic gaps between the poor and very wealthy. The particular forms and ways that these general themes take shape and play out vary depending upon the history, culture, geography, and length of colonization for both the colonized and colonizing countries.

As suggested in the section on postmodernism, many women in so-called Third World or developing countries receive employment in information technology industries or because of technological developments such as satellites that permit rapid data transmission over large geographic distances. The United States, Western Europe, and Japan house the corporate headquarters, owners, and decision-makers of these global, multinational corporations that uses technology to roam the globe and use women in offshore, formerly colonized, and developing nations as cheap sources of labour. Transcending boundaries of time and space, the new technologies aid corporations in dispersing work around the globe to exploit sexual and racial divisions of labour.

Information technology, satellites, and computerization become the glue that holds the global networks within a company together and permits them to function smoothly and efficiently. The clothing company Benetton exemplifies this:

At the Italian headquarters is a computer that is linked to an electronic cash register in every Benetton shop; those which are far away, like Tokyo and Washington are linked via satellite. Every outlet transmits detailed information on sales daily, and production is continuously and flexibly adjusted to meet the preferences revealed in the market.

In contrast, the Internet has also been used to play a role in the coordination against capitalist imperialism, through cyberattacks on the World Trade Organization that hijacked its website and disabled its servers.

The IT industry itself uses subcontracted female labour in developing countries, particularly for software development. Western managements control the conduct of software development projects, using women from India, China, Mexico, Hungary, and Israel as programmers who are preferred as workers over those in developed countries because of their technical and English proficiency, relatively high roles of productivity, and relatively low costs of labour.

Telecommunications technologies ease the transmission of specifications and completed work between the workers in developing countries and client companies in the West.

The same factors of technical and language proficiency and low wage costs, coupled with satellite and telecommunications systems, have transformed the clerical industry. The financial services sector, in particular, has capitalized on computerization of clerical functions and the use of satellite and telecommunications functions to tap large pools of female clerical labour in Mexico, the Caribbean, Southeast Asia, China, India, and Ireland.

These examples from the garment, software, and clerical industries clearly demonstrate aspects of postcolonialism, in that control of the economies of developing countries remains in the hands of developed countries. They demonstrate patriarchal control since women, not men; in the developing countries become the sources of cheap labour. Language becomes an interesting feature that continues to tie former colony with colonizer.

Theoretically, satellites and telecommunications transcend geographical barriers and permit any developed country to use labour in any developing country. Practically, the former ties developed between colony and colonizer, including the language of the colonizer learned by the colonized during the period of colonization, means that former relationships continue in the neocolonial modern world. Does the conversion of some Indian universities to software factories exemplify this language connection in the IT world where English dominates?

CYBERFEMINISM EXAMINED

Originating partly in response to the very male and anarchic politics of cyberpunk, many members of both women's studies and the information technology communities noted the explicit fusion of gender with the emergent technologies of the information revolution in the world cyberfeminism. As the name suggests, cyberfeminism explores the ways that information technologies and the Internet provide avenues to liberate (or oppress) women. In the early 1990s the term cyberfeminism first began to be used in various parts of the world, with VNS Matrix, an Australian-based group of media-based artists, one of the first to employ it.

The individuals who defined cyberfeminism saw the potential of the Internet and computer science as technologies to level the playing field and open new avenues for job opportunities and creativity for women where absence of sexism, racism, and other oppression would serve as major contrasts between the virtual world and the real world:

Cyberfeminism: A woman-centered perspective that advocates women's use of new information and communications technologies of empowerment. Some cyberfeminists see these technologies as inherently liberatory and argue that their development will lead to an end to male superiority because women are uniquely suited to life in the digital age.

The early days of computer science and information technologies seemed to reflect these dreams. In 1980, women represented 37 percent of computer science majors. As the series of articles revisiting the early history of computing revealed, Ada Lovelace contributed to the development of the protocomputer, and Grace Hopper created the first computer language composed of words and invented virtual storage. Women performed calculations and wired hardware for the first digital electronic computer, ENIAC (Electronic Numerical Integrator and Computer).

In the late 1980s, a drastic change began to occur. Numbers of women majoring in computer science plummeted, coinciding with the restructuring of the capitalist system on a global scale and the rise of financial speculation permitted by the nonproductive economic investment in the new information technologies. As Millar and other cyberfeminist critics point out, the existing elites have struggled to seize control and stabilize the commercial potential of digital technologies, as well as their research and development. Discontinuity, speed, symbolic and linguistic spectacle, and constant change characterize information technology and digital discourse.

Although these characteristics of instability and indeterminacy, because of the changing technology, open the possibility for other changes in the social realm and power relations, it is unclear that information technologies and cyberculture will result in such social changes. The insidious nature of the gender paradox cues constantly coming from society, economics, and psychology make it very difficult for individuals to imagine less conventional understandings of maleness and femaleness. Despite their postmodern veneer of fragmentation, shifting identities, and speed, information technologies rest upon the power of science and technology to emancipate humans and a faith in abstract reason.

This chapter has used several feminist theoretical perspectives to examine the relationships among women, gender, and information technology. Each one of these perspectives might also be applied to aspects of what is being called cyberfeminism. Liberal feminism, building upon its Enlightenment roots, does not question the positivist approaches of science or information technologies. Some of the early cyberfeminists using liberal feminist approaches believed that information technologies would put women on an equal footing with men.

Today, liberal feminist approaches raise issues of women's equal access to digital hardware and the digital world. Socialist feminism rejects positivism and emphasizes that all knowledge and technologies, including information technologies, emanate from human beings and reflect human power and capitalist relationships. Socialist feminists raise the issues of class, in terms of who profits from and who loses from cybertechnology. African American feminism emphasizes the Eurocentric approach to technology as reflected in the development and control of information technologies by the northern and western continents, creating what is characterized as the racial "Digital Divide."

Cyberfeminists using existentialist and psychoanalytic approaches raise gender differences based on women's role as caregiver and on their socialization to remain connected with friends, workers, and families. Cyberfeminists cite women's use of the Internet, which equals that of men, and women's interest in and development of hardware, which lags significantly behind that of men, as examples of women's desire to remain connected.

Radical feminists would point out the potential use of IT to create alternative versions of reality and even to avoid interactions with men in the real world. Radical feminists also reveal oppression, pointing out that the Internet becomes a tool making women more vulnerable to men using it for ordering brides from developing countries, prostitution, cybersex, assumption of false identities, and pornography. Queer and transgender theories would sever prescriptive links between sex, gender, and sexual orientation, as evidenced when men assume female identities in chat rooms online.

Postmodern feminists would underline the fast, fragmented, and situation-dependent nature of information technologies and digital discourse and the impossibility of universalizing its use, design, or impact for all women. Postmodern perspectives may explain, at least partially, the lack of coherence and uncritical use of some feminist theories to support cyberfeminism. Some cyberfeminists see information technologies as liberatory, while others see them as oppressive towards women.

Postcolonial feminists, depending upon their country of origin and its colonial history, hold differing perspectives of cyberfeminism, united only by their marginal stance. Postcolonial feminists from India might highlight the widening gap between the software designers from one of their universities, now being converted to specialize in educating information technology workers, and the owners in the United States and England that control the software company.

Postcolonial feminists in Kenya might question when most people in their country will have electricity, let alone computers, in their homes, as the globalization of the IT industry continues. Currently, in my opinion, cyberfeminism uses aspects of different feminist theories to reflect many interactions among information technologies, women, and feminism. Until it achieves a more coherent theoretical framework, cyberfeminism might be characterized as a developing feminist theory.

6

Perspectives from Human Cognitive Development

This chapter extends feminist critiques of information technology (IT) by examining the development of children's processing of information; for example, the development of the representation, manipulation, and use of information and the goal is to construct a theoretical framework to guide feminist research in computer science and cognitive science. This framework reflects a feminist focus on connections rather than an androcentric focus on separation and distance and applies to the framework to the interface of children's thinking and their experiences on the Internet. Thus, this chapter will go beyond feminist critiques of current IT by outlining a fruitful direction that a feminist theory of IT informed by developmental perspectives might take.

Research on children has not been integrated well into feminist scholarship. Women's studies scholars address intersections of gender, race, ethnicity, class, and sexual orientation across a range of topics, including information technology. However, age typically is ignored, even though these intersections have a different effect on, and different issues for, babies, children, adolescents, young adults, and aging adults.

This is true also in the case of gender and IT. Most of the work in this area focuses on and privileges the perspectives and issues of young and middle-aged adults. Any work including children tends to focus on topics such as the effectiveness of educational software in schools and gender differences in computer practices.

The feminist transformation of computer information-processing models can suggest different designs in computer science, different AI systems, and different models of human-computer interactions and a feminist model that focuses on connections among information, connections between the knower and the phenomenon thought about, and nonlinear complex thinking. As it happens, these characteristics describe the sort of thinking and acquisition of knowledge that seem to occur when people use the Internet. Thus, by focusing on a topic compatible to feminism, the Internet, feminist models of thinking potentially could offer interesting new directions for studying human thought and designing AI systems in cognitive science.

In other words, the Internet, already an important topic in cognitive science, may serve as a fruitful project for the further development of a feminist cognitive science with respect to children and the Internet, to show how connections-based thinking might develop. Specifically, I suggest that the structure and functioning of the Internet might encourage cognitive structures and processes in children that focus on connections. In short, feminist models of cognitive science could capitalize on the connected nature of information on the Internet to a) explore an underexamined aspect of thinking and cognitive development, specifically, connections, and b) suggest Web site and Internet designs that encourage connected thinking even further.

Finally, by examining the socialization of children's thinking and to show that a developmental perspective can shed light on the societal implications of IT by examining the social construction of human cognition. By taking a feminist focus on connections in this chapter, I hope to stimulate the construction of a more complete theory of cognitive science that integrates the traditional emphasis on separation and linearity with the feminist emphasis on connections and networks of information.

That is, I focus on connections, not as a type of thinking separated from more traditional sorts of thinking, but as a step toward a broader and more adequate theory of cognition. Although it has been suggested that women may tend to think in connected ways more than do men, I give little attention to this issue in this chapter. Rather, I focus on neglected aspects of cognition-connections-that are addressed by feminist theory. Surely the thinking of both males and females has aspects involving connections.

COMPUTER AS METAPHOR FOR COGNITION

Before examining the computer as a traditional masculine metaphor for cognition and cognitive development, it is necessary to examine more generally how the study of cognitive development during childhood has been implicitly gendered. Metaphors derived from cultural constructions of masculinity have dominated the study of cognitive development. Four main categories of metaphor are development as argument, survival of the fittest, arrow, and building.

Argument depicts development as progress through conflict, for example, when a child's more advanced and less advanced concepts about the world conflict with each other. Survival of the fittest refers to competition, domination, competition, and hierarchy, as when the more advanced concept in the conflict eventually wins. The arrow metaphor indicates the directionality of development-a linear trajectory and progress through various points toward some predetermined goal (for example, an ideal adult).

The metaphor of building emphasizes linear, preplanned progress toward a superior, higher, more advanced level of thinking and implies the male domain of architecture. These metaphors "blend masculine imagery with a particular abstract, universal logic form." They highlight masculine themes such as "upward thrust, overcoming obstacles, inevitable progress and accession of the individual to a superior position." In contrast, developmentalists could have used feminist metaphors of development such as friendship, conversation, apprenticeship, and narrative that "highlight social interchange as both process and end point, the development of relational thought through a process of relatedness."

Feminist metaphors depict development as collaboration, mutual support, forming connections, cooperation, and flexible negotiation of complex (rather than simple linear) developmental routes. From feminist perspectives, outcomes are diverse and depend on children's social locations, goals, and possibilities and barriers in their contexts. Most research on cognitive development has implicitly used masculine metaphors rather than feminist ones.

A specific case of a prevalent masculine metaphor of reasoning is the use of the computer as a metaphor for rational thinking. Cognitive scientists involved in AI or simulations of human cognition have been fond of using IT metaphors to characterize thinking. Years ago, a telephone switchboard was a popular metaphor. A computer has been a main metaphor guiding the study of thinking and its development for the past twenty-five years. In this information-processing approach, thinking is likened to a computer. Cognitive scientists talk about the flow of information through the cognitive system. This flow begins with some "input," such as a written passage, a problem to be solved, or an event, into the human information-processing system.

The flow ends with an "output," which can be information stored in long-term memory, motor behaviour, speech, or a decision. Mental operations occur between input and output, and "control processes" or "executive functions," higher in the hierarchy, control these operations. These mental processes are similar in some ways to computer programs that accept information, perform certain operations on it, store the information, and produce output. More generally, both humans and computers manipulate symbols and transform input into output. Both are limited in the amount of information that can be attended to simultaneously and in the speed with which this information can be processed. The correspondence is, of course, only partial.

The circuitry of a computer is quite unlike the anatomy of the brain. Applications of the computer information-processing model to cognitive development during the past thirty years have produced evidence that with increasing age children become faster and more efficient at processing information, more in control as they develop problem-solving strategies, and more adept at linear thinking. Storage capacity and so-called working memory increase as well.

A feminist critique would point out that this view of thinking, focused on socially constructed masculinity, depicts the mind as disembodied, distanced, linear, objective, and decontextualized, just as "male" has been associated with "reason" more generally in Western philosophy. The mind, with its flow of information, seems separated from both body and context. This view reinforces the androcentric dualism of mind and body. Moreover, the metaphor depicts a rational mind, devoid of emotion. This mind develops in a linear trajectory toward an adult rational mind, as more efficient and more rational forms of thought win out over less efficient and less rational forms.

Finally, because the mind has no context, it is a universal mind with a view from nowhere. Thus, an AI device may appear to have no perspective, but in fact it implicitly has the perspective of its male designers in its emotionless and decontextualized processing of information, calculations, and applications of procedures. The mind does indeed seem gendered. Scholars such as Elizabeth Wilson have argued that computer models have been successful in psychology not because of the veridicality of the computer metaphor but because of its masculine assumptions about thinking.

The gender bias in information-processing models can be seen in computer programming. Sherry Turkle and Seymour Papert point out that typically the most valued programming style is the construction of a formal system of rules and hierarchies through the manipulation of abstract symbols, the control of a program through planning and mastery over the system. They note, "For some people in our study, what is exciting about computers is working within a rule-driven system that can be mastered in a top-down, divide-and-conquer way."

Moreover, "a distanced relationship with objects supports an analytic, rule, and plan-oriented style." Recent cognitive information-processing models are labeled connectionist, but are very unlike the connections emphasized by feminist approaches. The focus still is on competition among different neural (or computer) pathways and survival of the fittest pathway.

FEMINIST TRANSFORMATIONS OF COMPUTER AS METAPHOR FOR COGNITION

Feminist transformations of computer information-processing models can suggest different designs in computer science, different AI systems, and different human-computer interactions. In contrast to androcentric models of thinking, feminist epistemologies challenge the assumptions of objectivity, separation, and decontextualized knowledge. Applications of feminist epistemologies to cognitive science suggest a focus on connections among information, connections between the knower and the phenomenon thought about, and nonlinear complex thinking.

It is interesting that this feminist focus on connections, complexity, and nonlinear thinking describes the sort of thinking and acquisition of knowledge that seems to occur when using the Internet. Thus, by focusing on the Internet, feminist models of thinking potentially could be very compatible with computer science and offer fruitful new directions for studying human thought and designing AI systems. Most of the traditional information-processing models do not fully capture the sort of thinking involved in using the Internet. This section will explore some of these compatibilities between the Internet and a model of cognition and cognitive development based on feminist epistemologies and possibilities for feminist extensions.

Researchers largely have ignored the possibility that the structure and functioning of the Internet might encourage certain kinds of cognitive structures and processes in children. Most research on children and computers focuses on evaluating educational software, determining the effects of computer games on social and emotional development, evaluating computerized psychological assessments, examining gender bias in access to or use of computers, and designing effective computer learning environments.

For example, when used the key words children and computers in PsychINFO, a major data-base for articles in psychology and education, the one hundred most recent publications (i.e., since 2001) contained no articles on the basic cognitive operations involved in using the Internet, the focus of the current chapter. Given this gap in our knowledge, the present chapter will perform a task analysis of using Web sites and searching the Internet and identify the basic cognitive processes implied by this task analysis that should be examined in future research.

The organization of information on the Web resembles a network, or a roadmap, where multidirectional connections are what matter, rather than a linear (or even parallel-simultaneous) processing system. A task analysis suggests that when children search the Web for information they enter a highly interconnected set of sites. When navigating the Internet, they learn about the nature of links and how information connects from site to site. They also surely learn that there are different routes to the same site and that a given site can lead to various endpoints. In addition, the Internet requires the user to be interactive.

A child must make a decision, at each step, about which link to select next. The results of entering one link determine which links are available to be selected next. The user moves between material and around material quickly and easily, often in ways not possible in the physical world. Thus, the child and the Web have a reciprocal relationship. Children also may learn that mental actions are reversible. By clicking the Back button, the child returns to an earlier cognitive location and can even go Home again and start over.

Other aspects of the Internet are the high speed at which information is acquired, the enormous numbers of sites (or people, through e-mail) all over the world that one can reach in seconds, and anonymity. All these aspects of the Internet, along with a lack of information gatekeeping, raise new questions: Will children come to expect quick answers, consider knowledge to be a prepackaged commodity, or be unable to critically evaluate information from different sources, in this case Web sites?

For example, it may be more difficult to discriminate between an advertisement and a peer-reviewed research report on the Internet than in their printed versions. Given these characteristics of the human-Internet interface, which differs somewhat from older ways of acquiring information, it is surprising that little attention has been given to how the Internet might suggest a different model of thinking-either AI or simulations of human thought.

Hundreds of studies in developmental psychology have documented that to a great extent, children acquire concepts, habits of thought, and cognitive skills through activities partially shaped by cultural practices (such as parenting, schooling, gender roles, and play). Traditional theories of cognitive development have tended to assume Western androcentric ideals of separation of knower from known, objectivity, control of self and others, and linear thinking, as described earlier in the masculine metaphors. The focus has been on the physical world of objects, space, time, and causality. However, this has resulted in a restricted, biased model of cognitive development.

Certain kinds of thinking are slighted, particularly those developed when interacting with other people, especially in close relationships and in nurturing activities. In such activities, the focus is on connections: seeing connections among entities, events, and contexts; identifying others' thoughts and perspectives; thinking with others in collaborative activities; and immersing oneself in that which one is trying to understand, rather than separating from it.

Traditional, androcentric accounts of knowledge and its acquisition may have slighted these sorts of thinking, because in many cultures, they have been associated with feminine roles into which girls tend to be socialized. The proposed model of thinking that focuses on connections would provide a fruitful framework for studying the relations between the Internets and developing human minds. This proposed feminist transformation of the traditional information-processing model of mind as computer would provide a theoretical framework for an analysis of how the ability to think about connections both facilitates competent use of the Internet and is encouraged by the Internet.

INTERCONNECTED KNOWING

Much of my recent work in women's studies has been devoted to developing a theory of cognitive development that focuses on connections called interconnected knowing. It draws on feminist epistemologies, which expand the definition of knowledge to include connections. Children develop cognitively by thinking not only about the physical world but also about the social world. Human interaction is about connections.

What understanding about connections are learned when playing with dolls, playing house, talking with friends, taking care of a younger sibling, navigating the Internet, and learning in small collaborative groups? Such activities provide training in thinking about connections. Because many girls across a variety of cultures are socialized to engage in caretaking activities, either for younger siblings or dolls, a theory of interconnected knowing gives more attention to activities associated with females, typically slighted in current theories of cognitive development.

A theory of interconnected knowing could be seen as an example of "starting with the experience of females," as many females are encouraged to participate in certain activities during their socialization. Considerable evidence documents the socialization of a connection orientation in girls. Girls tend to be socialized to attend to relationships, contexts, and implications of their behaviour for other people. The effects of this socialization can be seen, for example, in the finding that many young women who major in science, or plan to, do so because of their connections to other people and their desire to help them.

There also is evidence that when girls are aggressive they tend to use relational aggressive tactics: gossiping about others or threatening to exclude them from social events, such as a birthday party. In addition, cultural norms against girls directly confronting others, as well as girls' desire to maintain their social group, lead to self-assertive talk that meshes a girl's needs with those of other people. However, it is interesting that boys in settings requiring solidarity outcomes also engage in this style of talk. Thus, a connections orientation is less about gender per se than about encouraged activities and the goals in a particular setting.

What if one assumed the world is interconnected, rather than populated with decontextualized separate objects? Taking such a stance when constructing a model of cognition, including artificial intelligence, leads to a model that looks different from our current models of cognition and AI based on androcentric assumptions of distance between knower and known and of reasoning about the physical world rather than the social world. The metaphors of interconnected thinking are web, fugue, tapestry, dialogue, and the Internet. They also express Ellin Scholnick's feminist metaphors of friendship, conversation, apprenticeship, and narrative described earlier.

In my model, thinking is interconnected in four ways:

1. Thinkers see connections in the world. The phenomenon to be understood is connected to its context; everything is situated rather than isolated.

2. The knower is connected to the phenomenon to be understood rather than distanced from it.
3. The knower's mental representations of knowledge are interconnected among themselves and with emotion, the body, and behaviour. Dichotomies between, for example, mind and body, are questioned.
4. The thinker is connected to his or her social context, including other knowers, during the collaborative co-construction of knowledge.

This model, based on feminist epistemologies, clearly differs from the traditional male view of an objective, autonomous thinker, distanced from a decontextualized object and separated from other knowers, who dominates the object and ignores emotions. In contrast, in a feminist model of cognitive science, thinking is always situated. There is no view from nowhere. During development, children acquire (construct) knowledge about connections through connections.

This feminist model of thinking is compatible with the type of thinking necessary for exploring Web sites, which in turn provides useful considerations for Web site design:

1. Through links, buttons connect to other parts of a Web site or to other Web sites. A search is a journey through a massive set of links.
2. A user actively selects and enters a site and interacts with that site and other sites. A reciprocal relationship exists between children and the Internet as they initiate a search, respond to the produced link, enter another link, and so on.
3. A child may construct a mental map of the site and its relations to other sites. Emotion is involved in that a user is interested in and values some links over others.
4. Social interaction with other people (e.g., playmates, parents, or coworkers) in the immediate environment while surfing the Web or communicating with other people electronically may shape the child's construction of knowledge on the Internet.

Web sites and other IT designs (for example, AI systems in cognitive science) make assumptions about what kind of thinking is important and what is important to think about. Such systems tend to be constructed by and oriented toward the main users: middle-class white males. In contrast, intelligence systems or models based on interconnected thinking would focus on aspects of thinking-connections-typically considered relatively unimportant and thus slighted in male-based systems. This theoretical model provides new theoretical directions for cognitive science accounts of the Internet. It also advances feminist accounts of knowledge by linking feminist epistemology to specific cognitive practices in daily life, particularly, using the Internet.

ASPECTS OF INTERCONNECTED KNOWING

The four features of interconnected knowing presented above describe four locations of interconnected thinking-among components of the world, between self and world, within self, and between self and other people. Interconnected knowing also can be characterized in another way, in terms of six aspects of such thinking, regardless of its location. I now will describe these six aspects.

First, the interconnected-knowing model emphasizes contextual-relational reasoning. Connections with contexts are important in feminist scholarship. For example, Carol Gilligan describes moral reasoning in which judgments are made in terms of people's relationships with other people in specific contexts rather than on the basis of decontextualized universal principles about an autonomous person. Caring and responsibility to others become more important than issues of justice and individual rights, emphasized by traditional approaches.

Contextual-relational reasoning also can be seen in Barbara McClintock's scientific reasoning and methods. This Nobel Prize-winning geneticist examined how the context of a gene (i.e., other genes, the entire cell, the whole organism of which it is a part, and features of the environment such as droughts) affects its expression and functioning. In her view, genes "are organized functional units, whose very function is defined by their position in the organization as a whole." The outcomes of situated-contextual thinking may be knowledge that is concrete, situation-specific, unstable, relative, and tentative rather than abstract, universal, absolute, and certain. A fact may pertain only to particular circumstances. Particularities of persons and situations are valued.

The organization of Web sites implicitly conveys information about relations among sets of information as much as about the sets of knowledge themselves. In fact, the very words link and site map emphasize connections. And it is always comforting to return to the Home page. However, connections could easily be made much more explicit in Web designs. For example, the Web index or directory usually is presented as a hierarchical list with subsections, but it could be presented as a matrix or roadmap, so that the relations among the parts would be clearer.

Some parts would be linked strongly, because they are highly related conceptually; other links would be weaker. Some links may be related only through a common link. If one applies contextual-relational reasoning to Web site design, the focus would be on relations among components of the Web site and among links. As noted earlier, because of their gender socialization, many women and girls may be more comfortable with working with a Web site based on interconnected thinking, because it is compatible with their concepts of the social world.

A second characteristic of a Web site designed from an interconnected-knowing perspective is that the site would encourage thinking about complex networks of multidirectional causal connections. This is closely related to the first characteristic described above. From a feminist perspective, to know an entity or event is to perceive its dynamic causal connections within itself and with the world. The world is more complex than would appear from more linear models. Any event has many causes and, in turn, affects many other entities and events with which it is connected. An example from classic work in feminism is feminist biologists' critique of the "master molecule" view that DNA controls and directs cellular activity; they contend that a more interactive, multidirectional model of influences is more accurate.

Another example of a complex bidirectional causal model is including the contributions of the egg to conception, as well as those of the sperm. The sperm is not the only active partner. Egg and sperm are mutually active partners in a complex system. A final example of top-down models is that cognitive scientists often speak of central "control processes" or "executive functions." The problem is that if one believes that entity 1 "dominates" entity 2, then one is more likely to focus IT designs on the activities of entity 1 than on the contributions of entity 2 that facilitate the activities of entity 1. Thus, models based on domination and subordination presents a biased view of the world.

A Web site design based on the feminist model of interconnected thinking would encourage thinking about complex bidirectional causal connections among information components on the site. Children go through several developmental phases before they fully understand these complex connections, such as dynamic systems characterizing ecological systems. A third characteristic of interconnected thinking is that knowledge is constructed through reciprocity, connecting, and dialogue between knower and known. Knowing is interconnected not only because what is known is interconnected but also because the knower is connected with the known.

If a child is interconnected with the phenomenon to be known, rather than separated from it, then there are implications for the process of knowing. The knower becomes immersed in that which is to be known, rather than independent of it and distanced from it. As the immunologist Anna Brito said, "Most importantly, of course, you must identify with what you're doing. You must identify totally. If you really want to understand about a tumor, you've got to be a tumor."

In addition, as geneticist Barbara McClintock remarked, "I know every plant in the field. I know them intimately, and I find it a great pleasure to know them;" a person needs to "get inside an idea," "listen to the material," and develop a "feeling for the organism." A friendship metaphor seems apt. Knowledge gradually emerges from the interaction between the knower and the known, much like in a conversation. Dialogue is an epistemological tool. Knowing is an active, constructive process in which neither the known nor the knower dominates. Knowledge acquisition is quintessentially an interactive process.

A Web site designed to draw on reciprocity and dialogue would encourage the user to enter the Web site space and immerse her in the various components in an interactive way. Turkle and Papert found that many people (more often women) use a style of writing computer programs that is very interactive and negotiative, with the programmer starting in a certain direction but making adjustments in response to feedback. Such programmers "have goals, but set out to realize them in the spirit of a collaborative venture with the machine."

The computer is more like a harpsichord than a hammer. Connections and relationships are primary. Similarly, on an Internet search a person might change her intended direction when her initial direction takes her to sites on relevant topics that she had not considered before. In contrast, as described earlier, traditional masculine programming approaches tend to be more linear and hierarchical, with the process planned ahead of time and the programmer or Web navigator in more control.

Fourth, interconnected knowing emphasizes the social aspects of cognition. Interconnected thinking is social in two ways: It addresses connections and relationships, and it values the applications of cognition to social problems and goals. Of interest is how cognitive systems-natural or artificial-can be used to understand other people, to build social bonds, and to work with other people to improve the quality of life. In one interview study, many women computer scientists and engineers described getting pleasure in their work from problems or activities pertaining to someone else's enjoyment and involvement; for example, enhanced communication among people, making technology more accessible to people, and collaborating with others on computer projects.

In contrast, men were more likely to talk about obtaining pleasure from the technology itself. There is significant evidence for children's understanding of the social world. The understanding of social connections is especially evident in children's growing awareness of recursive thinking, such as "he's thinking that she's thinking that he's thinking..." To my knowledge, few AI systems simulate reasoning about the social world, about the causes of other people's behaviour and their relations with each other. In interconnected thinking, knowledge about the social world is as important as knowledge about the physical world, mathematical calculations, or pure logical systems.

Unlike most models of cognition that begin with reasoning about the physical world and then expand the application of this reasoning to the social world, the interconnected thinking model takes the social world as its starting point. Research could examine how children use computers to communicate with friends over the Internet, as much as for computer games centered on violence.

One social cognitive skill that would be useful for Web site design is the ability to take the perspective of other people, in this case the user. The designs of many Web sites are very egocentric. I am reminded of this every time I search for faculty members on Web sites at various universities.

On some Web sites, clicking on the category faculty produces a search engine to find faculty at that institution, and on some Web sites the same choice results in information about benefits, leave policies, and such, intended for faculty members at that university. Similarly, the button labels of some university Home pages give no clue to how to find academic departments. Designers' selection of which categories to use as buttons on a Web site calls for great attention to understanding other people's perspectives.

Fifth, people co-construct knowledge together. Understanding is often a social, negotiated, and shared activity involving the co-construction of knowledge. In other words, an epistemological community constructs knowledge. Knowledge of the world often comes from cognitive interaction with others. Discussing our experiences with others shapes our interpretation of our experiences. Valued activities during co-construction include sharing ideas, building on each other's ideas, and nurturing and supporting the ideas of others. Adversarial, argumentative discourse is less valued than cognitive reciprocity and a narrative discourse.

Although we know that children often play with the Internet in small groups and collaborative teams in the workplace often design Web pages together, only a few studies have examined such collaborative activities. One study, for example, found that preschoolers interacted with peers in complex ways when playing at the computer together. Another study reported gender differences in interaction in a MUD (multiuse domain)-an online site designed to encourage identity exploration and peer interaction. Among preadolescents who did not know each other, pairs of boys interacted through action, rapid changes, and playful exchanges.

Pairs of girls interacted mainly through written dialogue. Interactions of girl-boy pairs were in between these two styles. Thus, the gendered social context of computer activities affects a child's activities on the computer. Socialized gender roles appear to influence such activities. Collaborative activities often involve a particular kind of social relationship: scaffolding. When parents teach a young child how to navigate the Internet, they scaffold, or support, the child's attempts at this activity. The parent gives hints, prompts, and suggestions. As children follow a parent's mind through the process of solving a problem, they learn to use those patterns of thought.

The child gradually takes on more responsibility in the activity, and the parent gradually withdraws assistance as the child internalizes the skill and learns to function without help. In one study, educational software for ten- and eleven-year-olds was most effective when it was based on this notion of scaffolding and collaborative interactions, with flexible scaffolding that could gradually be faded out and individualized to each user. I will expand on the internalization of computer-based activities in the next section of this chapter.

Sixth, in interconnected thinking, diversity is attended to and valued. Race, gender, class, sexuality, and physical ability all contribute to the construction of knowledge. Each child is unique as a knower, because she or he occupies a unique place in a sociohistorical-physical setting. Situated knowledge is always diverse. Thus, knowers may differ in the particular search route they take. Moreover, it is likely that computer scientists of various social positions would construct different sorts of Web sites. For example, certain women-of-colour feminist epistemologies describe how oppressed people often develop a double vision; to survive, they must understand and predict the behaviour of the dominant group as well as hold their own perspective.

Understanding other people involves an awareness of how their diverse experiences, formed by gender, race, and social class, and so forth; contribute to their attitudes, beliefs, and behaviors. Such knowledge may contribute to the construction of less egocentric Web sites. Moreover, for children, the Internet is potentially a window to diverse cultures internationally and to communication with people from many cultures. Related to this, one issue within cyberfeminism concerns how people can experiment with alternative identities and forms of interaction in cyberspace.

Finally, a very different implication of the focus on diversity in interconnected knowing is that a universal system of logic need not be the only goal of AI systems. In fact, a main challenge of designing AI systems is to create a system that can deal with diverse content, situations, and goals. In summary, a model of thinking based on feminist epistemology suggests new ways to conceptualize the human-computer interface. I have noted several ways in which structure of the Internet is compatible with interconnected knowing; however, these six aspects of interconnected knowing suggest new questions for future research on what children think about and how they learn, especially as a result of their experiences on the Internet.

INFLUENCES OF THE INTERNET

The Internet not only fits well with the interconnected thinking that all children bring to the computer in varying degrees, but also may encourage interconnected thinking. Next I demonstrate how a developmental perspective can inform feminist studies of computer science, especially those focused on the social implications of technology, by suggesting a process by which the computer can influence thinking. Sociocultural developmental theory addresses the cultural, social, and historical forces that contribute to the development of individual minds.

This theory is compatible with feminist theory and provides an account of how cultural practices, including technology, shape minds in particular ways valued by that culture. The theory can suggest ways to study how children's experiences with the Internet can socialize interconnected thinking. According to this theory, thinking is always social. By engaging in cultural rituals, institutions, artifacts, and technologies, children develop cognitively. Technologies such as writing instruments, computers, and calculators shape minds in particular ways.

According to sociocultural theory, children of today, who gather much of their information over the Internet may have a different way of thinking than did the previous generation, just as the construction of a system of writing changed the thinking of a much earlier generation in human history. Children develop cognitively by engaging in cultural practices, including those involving IT settings, with a variety of adults and older peers. Thus, "it takes a village...." In short, entering the Internet is a cultural practice; a cultural community provides this tool and invites children (to various degrees, according to gender, race, class, and nationality) to use it.

One piece of evidence that computer-based activities affect thought is that practice on computer games leads to improvements in children's spatial skills, such as mentally rotating an object to a different orientation and dealing with two-dimensional images of a hypothetical two- or three-dimensional space. What is lacking, however, is research on how the structure and functioning of the Internet encourages particular ways of thinking and acquiring knowledge during childhood.

The experience of navigating the Internet may instill particular ways of seeking information and using that information. The organization of a Web site, for example, may convey a particular way of structuring information and thus organizing the world into categories. Many different ways of organizing a Web site can convey the same information, but they encourage different thought processes by, for example, including different categories of buttons and site indexes. According to sociocultural theory, as children explore Web sites they internalize the cognitive organization of the Web site and the form of the interaction between self and Web site.

Once these are internalized they become part of the child's thinking. What was external becomes internal (mental). As a result of internalization, the map of links and their connections on the Internet could become a mental map. Or moving forward and backward on the Internet could become the cognitive skill of reversing a mental operation, a watershed developmental accomplishment observed by Piaget. If the computer program, computer game, or Web design expresses socialized stereotypic male qualities of linearity, separation, distance, autonomy, violence, and control, then those cognitive structures and processes may be internalized.

However, we know that many girls resist some aspects of this technology. For example, many reject the aggressive video games so favored by boys and may prefer to use computers for communication. Thus, sociocultural theory suggests a dynamic relation between the Internet and thinking.

The organization and functioning of the Internet may encourage particular types of thinking, but children who think in various ways partly because of socialization differences may resist or fit into the Internet structure to varying degrees. My interest in these differences is less in whether they fall along gender lines than in encouraging the study of interconnected thinking which contrasts with traditional androcentric "objective" thought.

Sociocultural developmental theory also addresses one important issue in the information technology workplace: collaborative problem-solving teams. Schools that encourage collaborative activities in the classroom and those with more traditional hierarchical structures and individual problem-solving may encourage different sorts of thinking in children, because children internalize the ways of conversing and thinking of people around them. If girls, because of their gender socialization, tend to choose collaborative activities, they will obtain more experience with the kind of thinking required by such activities and thus may become particularly expert at the sorts of collaborative problem-solving now needed in the IT workforce.

Still another issue about the effects of the Internet on society concerns differences in race and social class, as well as gender, that may lead to inequities in the extent to which children develop the sorts of cognitive skills that are advantageous for using the Internet in school and later in the workplace. Children are more likely to use computers if they are white rather than African American or Hispanic and from families of high income and education.

Taking a cognitive developmental perspective can deepen and expand feminist epistemology. A developmental perspective points to the childhood origins of traditional and connected cognition. It is likely that children develop a broad, complex, integrated, cognitive system with intertwined interconnected-knowing components and separated-knowing components. This model breaks down the dichotomy between the two; they are integral aspects of a larger system and may work together to help children construct a meaningful representation of the world.

The interconnected-knowing model also provides accounts of how knowledge is acquired through socially constructed gendered experiences of daily life. This model enriches feminist epistemologies that turn to social epistemological communities and social experiences for the foundations of knowledge. Adults and children together co-construct knowledge. In this construction of knowledge, human interconnections are as important as separations; relationships are as important as autonomy; reciprocity and dialogue are as important as domination and control; and nonlinear narrative thinking is as important as linear thinking.

A cognitive developmental perspective can also enrich feminist research on gender and IT. I have argued that the nature of the Internet can provide a wedge for feminist accounts of IT. Because interconnected thinking is compatible with the structure of the Internet, the former can provide theoretical concepts and tools for constructing a feminist theory of cognitive science. By building on current connected aspects of Web sites and Internet searches, it is possible to develop these connected aspects even further.

Integrating feminist models with traditional models may produce a computer science or cognitive science that reflects not only experiences associated with males but also the experiences associated with females. By highlighting what has been ignored in the past-in this case, human interactions, connections, and relationships-I have demonstrated that a feminist account can go beyond critiques of cognitive science and begin to construct a model of cognition based on feminist perspectives.

THE SOCIAL IMPLICATIONS OF AN INFORMATION SOCIETY

The development of technology is difficult to predict - but how it will be used and what the impact of it will be on society are almost impossible to forecast. As we have seen, it is easy to assume over-optimistically that the most desirable possible scenario will inevitably come about. In the absence of government intervention, the most likely outcome is that market forces will largely determine the use society makes of IT and the impact IT has on society. Inevitably, on this basis, there will be a tendency for the most affluent societies (such as the United States), and the most affluent members of societies (the prosperous and the powerful), to make most use of the technology for their own benefit.

Under the impact of market forces such changes - responding to individual consumer demand fostered by profit-maximizing multinational corporations - may have unanticipated effects which affect society as a whole and may cost it dear in terms of environmental effects or the impact on social stability. This chapter attempts to consider some possible effects of this sort and the extent to which they can and should be controlled by government on behalf of the community as a whole in a democratic society.

In this new century it is clear that these problems will not be contain-able within national boundaries - given the impact of a global economy and global communication networks - so that any action required will inevitably have an international aspect if it is to be effective.

LEISURE AND THE HOME

In many ways, especially economically, the biggest impact of new information and communication technologies has been in the entertainment industry. Conventional cinema and broadcasting has gradually made increasing use of digital techniques in the preparation of special effects, cartoon features, the processing of news and the like. The net effects of all this, however, are arguably quite small compared with the massive impact of television and similar products on home life and the pattern of leisure activities.

Television, besides creating a multi-billion pound new global industry, has had a massive impact - making the family consumption of leisure industry products in their own home a central feature of social life. More recently massive investments have been made in the delivery of entertainment to the home, often using digital techniques. Digital CD-ROM has replaced older analogue recording technologies for music, necessitating the wholesale replacement of domestic collections of records and gramophones with hi-fis, Walkmans, and the like.

The development of video recorders has enabled families and individuals to decide what entertainment products to consume, and when, to a much greater extent. The provision of cable television, the development of satellite broadcasting, and the conversion of terrestrial, cable and satellite broadcasting to digital technology have all made available a greater choice of television channels at the cost of massive expenditure on infrastructure by the companies concerned (satellites, cables, etc.) and on new receiving equipment by the families concerned.

The reducing real cost of reception equipment, the mushrooming availability of myriads of recordings and multiple broadcast channels, the development of specialist interactive multi-media products such as 'zap it' computer games - appealing to small boys of all ages - has led to a further change: a move from family-group home consumption of entertainment products to individual consumption on different consoles at different times in different rooms (or even on the move).

It is easy to jump to conclusions as to what the social impact of such technological changes must be. Thus critics of television and other home entertainments have decried the decline of community life and creativity implicit in the abandonment of collective and relatively spontaneous local activities such as football clubs, pub sing-songs, allotments and local produce shows in favour of the passive viewing of professional sports, pop-videos and gardening programmes.

More recently teenage violence has been blamed upon inappropriate role models offered by pop songs, violent video games and horror films consumed by children unsupervised by their over-indulgent parents. Alternatively (and paradoxically sometimes simultaneously), a vision of a new generation of passive, isolated and socially inadequate 'couch potatoes' or 'geeks' has been painted. There has been much serious research on these issues, some of which is much less pessimistic and certainly more complicated in its conclusions than that of the critics referred to above. What is perhaps cheering and fits in with one of the themes of this book is the diversity of use to which domestic technologies are put in different homes.

Rather than a picture of passive and uniform consumption of pre-digested experiences, much research suggests that televisions, microwaves or personal computers can all be used to support radically different lifestyles. The same television programme may be treated as background filler, the subject of derision, a source of a useful minor piece of information on a topic far removed from its main theme, or as a spur to developing a new interest outside the home. With a sophisticated and multi-purpose piece of technology such as a personal computer, it is almost impossible to predict how it will be treated - as an educational resource for a child, as father's new hobby, or as a business tool for mother.

EDUCATION AND INFORMATION TECHNOLOGY

In the educational sphere it is clear that the potential for a radical transformation of learning using the new technology is as yet unrealized, even in countries such as the United States and the United Kingdom where the use of these technologies is most advanced. In many poorer countries it is possible that the use of IT could help to bridge the educational gap between them and richer areas of the world; but such a project would require an imaginative use of resources by the world community, which is perhaps unlikely in current circumstances.

In this section we shall examine the potential use of IT in

education and then consider the problems of moving from the present restricted use of the technology to a more full-blooded employment of these resources. Finally we shall consider the potentially disruptive effects of such a development. Modern IT offers the possibility of a learner's paradise in which not only can exciting multi-media educational materials be created, but they can be made to interact with the learner and be available just when and where the learner requires them - anytime, anywhere in the world.

The very best teachers can design materials and be available to tutor students anywhere in the world - in person if required. For more advanced students and teachers the resources of the world's libraries could be available electronically on-line and global seminars held to discuss work in progress. The technical systems already exist to implement such a vision. Consider the quality and interest of CD-ROMs already available, such as the Encarta Encyclopedia, and imagine greater and more coordinated efforts applied to all the basic areas of the curriculum. Materials are already constructed linking text, pictures and video and presented on CD-ROM or websites.

Hypertext links can be made available to enable any part of the text to be further explained. Batteries of objective test questions can be made available with which learners can assess themselves (or be assessed by third parties). The British Open University already has decades of experience of constructing high-quality learning materials which, in this case, combine written learning modules, broadcast or videoed television programmes, computer-marked objective test questions and, in some cases, on-line tuition and conferencing facilities as well as more conventional methods.

Already global groups of scholars discuss issues on-line - at present mainly in text-based forums - but videoconferencing facilities are technically possible and used from time to time. Project Gutenberg is steadily making available the texts of more and more classics of world literature and philosophy available on-line, whilst increasingly the contents of museums, archives and specialist libraries are available on the World Wide Web. (The catalogues of all the major academic libraries are already accessible - the texts to which they refer could also technically be made available.)

The advantages of making massive quantities of educational material available globally over the web and reorganizing educational systems so that individual learners can access it more or less as required seem obvious to the author. Much evidence shows that the optimum conditions for learning are when the learner perceives the need for the required information or skill and can use or practise his or her knowledge immediately. Global productivity should soar as the latest innovations and techniques become available more rapidly and can be utilized by a better-educated workforce. Hopefully the spread of mutual knowledge and increased communication will enhance international understanding.

A further possibility raised by these uses of technology is that most of such learning could take place in learners' own homes or workplaces. Schools and universities could exist largely as meeting places for such activities as sports and laboratory sessions which require physical contact, and as administrative centres for staff who would, however, largely work from home, like the students. It is instructive to consider why such developments have been slow to materialize - and may never do so! The obvious barriers to such developments are economic, but in the long run the major barriers may well be social, organizational and political.

The economic barriers include, of course, the need for a massive communications infrastructure linking all educational institutions (or homes), investment in hardware and software for each student and in the development of appropriate educational materials (including scanning the con tents of libraries into databases). Although appearing to be an enormous proposition, certainly entailing the expenditure of billions of pounds worldwide, this does not appear to be a major problem in the long term.

As we have seen, the infrastructure is likely to be created for entertainment and commercial purposes in any event and, if desired, specific educational expenditure could be justified out of cost savings on premises and staff (fewer should be required since much duplication of effort in course-development and delivery could be saved) and in terms of the greater cost-effectiveness of new-style learning compared with outmoded chalk and talk 'school' methods of learning.

Social barriers are much more likely to be a problem. In particular the 'baby-sitting' functions of the schools system might come to the fore if it was seriously proposed to go over in whole or in part to a system of home learning. Millions of working parents would not be enthused by the prospect of arranging supervision for their children's learning sessions - even though remote surveillance of the children's input to the computer could be set up! From an educational point of view, the ability to work and live in a group is something that is difficult to build into individual distance learning programmes.

Another social barrier to the effective implementation of such learning systems is, of course, teachers' concepts of their role and their technical competence to operate such new systems. One reason for the slow adoption of IT in schools and universities is that IT has been seen by most teachers as a technical area to be taught and employed by someone else. Most teachers graduated before computers were seen as an essential learning tool for all students, and relatively little in-service training has been provided in most school systems to remedy this attitude.

Organizational barriers to such a scheme are perhaps too many to list, but they include the important consideration that whilst from a learner's point of view it might be highly desirable to be taught electronically by the best institution in the world - every business student might aspire to an MBA awarded by the Harvard Business School, every classics student might seek an Oxford MA - the rest of the educational world might be less than overjoyed at the prospect of redundancy. Furthermore, elite institutions may wish to retain an exclusive posture and status and to concentrate on research rather than teaching. Legal and financial issues such as copyright and the need to levy fees to finance activities also restrict institutions' willingness to make their learning materials available on the World Wide Web.

Political barriers have been left to last, but they are far from least. We have already seen the resistance which parents, teachers and educational institutions might raise to the changes outlined; these may pale into insignificance to those which politicians and nationalists might endorse. Although it has been suggested that the economic resource problem should not be too large, it is clear that politicians frequently find it difficult to make large expenditures on public facilities. Extra expenditure might involve additional taxes or borrowing - even if, in the longer run, such expenditure may more than justify itself. If the justification involves closing local schools and making some teachers redundant, then the problem would be reinforced.

Still more serious, from the point of view of many politicians, is the loss of control over the curriculum, which the concept of a global educational network involves. Whilst there may be a measure of consensus over the mathematics and physics curriculum worldwide, would fundamentalist politicians in Alabama or Iran be happy to see their biology students learning about evolution in a course from Cambridge or MIT? Still more controversial are matters of history and geography in which a Russian, a Serbian or a Chinese perspective might differ radically from that of a US or a British course.

Finally in this brief consideration of the impact of IT on education we return to the issue of the role of IT in education in poorer countries. Here the case for implementing modern IT-based systems for learning is, if anything, stronger because most (but not all) of these countries have a severe shortage of skilled and knowledgeable teachers, lack adequate conventional educational institutions and could probably achieves a higher benefit from the same expenditure on such resources. The problems of implementation are, however, much greater, a fundamental problem clearly being the lack of financial resources to make the investment required. Even if the technical kit was directly donated by richer countries, the recipients may lack adequate electricity supplies, and the technical and managerial know-how, to install and maintain such systems. There is a danger that expensive equipment will rust idly away when technologically simpler solutions (e.g. subsidizing school textbook production) might be much more effective. Thus considerable thought needs to be given to ensuring that any information technology introduced is accompanied by skills training and the provision of an adequate supporting infrastructure. However, telecommunications companies from richer countries might be induced to collaborate with donor governments in developing potentially enormous markets in these areas. As in richer countries political problems may be the biggest obstacle to the use of IT in education. Many politicians may well see proposals to give all their schoolchildren access to the web as a plot to subvert national or religious values.

The predominance of English as a language on the web is not only a barrier for users in non-English-speaking countries but may also be seen as a device to undermine a national linguistic, literary and historical heritage. Last, but not least, amongst the perhaps unspoken political objections to the web may be resistance to the democratic values predominant upon the web and the opportunities it presents for free discussion and social and political activism.

CULTURE AND CYBERSPACE

The issues raised in the previous section about the impact of the web on national cultures deserve some further exploration and may perhaps be presented more bluntly. For optimists, the net represents a new stage in the development of human culture. This global culture, existing in 'cyberspace', enables human beings across the planet to share and invent new 'virtual realities', to be free and to communicate via new forms of art, and to collaborate in the development of scientific understanding and new technological developments.

For pessimists, the net is one more part of a process whereby American capitalism imposes a commercialized and vul-garized English-speaking culture of pop songs, pornography, block-buster films, jeans, hamburgers and commercial profiteering on a previously much more diverse and culturally sophisticated world. Each side of this argument will be presented and some attempt made to arbitrate, but the final judgement must be left to the reader.

The concept of global civilization, in which 'cyberspace' (the hypothetical electronic reality within which understanding, communication and activity on a global electronic net takes place) is the dominant feature of human culture, was probably first popularized by the science fiction writer William Gibson. He described it as:

> A consensual hallucination experienced daily by billions of legitimate operators, in every nation, by children being taught mathematical concepts... A graphic representation of data abstracted from the banks of every computer in the human system. Unthinkable complexity...

His novels are interesting in being far from 'computopias'. The future society dominated by the net is, in some respects, far from ideal, being still full of conflict, inequality, violence and subject to the power of large corporations. But it is a future in which technical knowledge and competence leads to personal power and effectiveness: the individual can make a difference. It is also a future in which national boundaries and geography seem of very limited importance.

In the future it seems likely that most people (in the richer parts of the world at least) will spend most of their day learning or working at a computer and also spend much of their leisure time interacting with computers or television monitors. If all these monitors are basically part of a global net using similar software and drawing upon a more or less common pool of data, then the social and cultural implications of all this seem both undeniably large and difficult to predict.

Commentators such as Rheinghold (1992) have stressed the potential importance of 'virtual reality' technologies. Three-dimensional graphic depictions of reality can be made to interact with one or more human participants, perhaps through specially designed helmets (which enable the display to respond to the participant's angle of vision) and gloves, or a joystick which enables participants to manipulate imaginary objects in the display. Most readers will have played computer games, which work on similar principles.

At their most realistic such technologies have been used to train firemen, astronauts and pilots to respond to life-like emergencies on simulations of actual equipment. (Viewers of Star Trek will be familiar with the 'Holodeck' in which the crew interact with computer holograms indistinguishable from reality - perhaps the ultimate expression of this idea.) The more interactive and realistic computer data is, arguably the more addictive it becomes, and the less easy it is for participants in the system to distinguish 'reality' from the contents of the screens before them. Conversely this type of presentation of data is undoubtedly effective in conveying an understanding of alien situations or the principles behind dynamic models.

In the arts 'video installations' have already sold for large sums in art galleries. Computer-generated graphics and special effects play an increasing role in the presentation of films and television programmes. Just as photography became accepted as an art form and immensely influenced other graphic arts in the nineteenth century, so it is to be expected that computer-generated displays will both influence art and be seen as a legitimate and major form of artistic expression in the twenty-first century. The use of mathematically generated 'fractal' displays has already proved influential.

Already electronically generated music is seen as a legitimate part of both popular and serious music. There have been suggestions that the great artists of the twenty-first century will be computer 'games' designers. Indeed the distinction between film and computer game may well disappear as the century progresses, and each member of the 'audience' will be able to 'customize' many imaginative interactive audio-visual presentations by (for instance) language, background, desired main characters, and preferred outcome. (Already DVD film tracks are produced in multiple language versions and can be indexed and accessed in various ways rather than merely played straight through.)

The use of the net in academic enquiry and debate has already been referred to. It can also be used to generate collaborative research teams (perhaps dispersed across the globe) to mount new enquiries, and to publicize new scientific discoveries and technological innovations. For that matter there are many 'alt.' (=alternative) discussion groups which seek to discuss and perhaps develop new forms of social cooperation. Hence it is possible enthusiastically to endorse the development of cyberspace as the herald of a new global society in which enlightened individuals from across the globe cooperate in a democratic (if not anarchic) fashion to build a better life for all.

The academic origins of the Internet and its growth in the hands of well-intentioned private hobbyists have helped to generate an individualistic and optimistic 'net-culture' to which we referred earlier. It is natural to envisage the growth of the net as bringing about more of the same - individualism and creativity thriving across the globe. However, it is possible to be much less optimistic about the likely future of the net if we consider that it is now moving into a new era of commercialization. As we have seen, the driver towards a massive expansion of the net in the twenty-first century is likely to be the prospect of profit from e-commerce.

Particularly as far as ordinary individuals are concerned, they are likely to be interactive users only in the sense of using the net for electronic shopping and downloading entertainment (which may be interactive in a rather pre-programmed sense). Already the most visited site on the Internet has been said to be Playboy magazines. In the future it seems likely that supermarket sites, such as the one Britain's huge Tesco chain is already operating, will be the most used on the web, perhaps contributing to the downfall of small 'craft' producers and retailers.

The great majority of Internet users and sites are, at present, American. This dominance seems unlikely to change in the foreseeable future. The slickest and often most useful and entertaining websites tend to be commercial US enterprises selling US-branded consumer goods and US cultural goods - videos, films, books. As with the worldwide film industry, the US industry can invest larger sums in development than any other because of the size of their home market, and then export at virtually zero additional cost. In the sphere of information goods the US is at a considerable advantage over most European countries and Japan because (US) English is the world's leading second language and the language of aerospace, computing, pop music and international commerce.

Consider the USA's success in dominating broadcast media, publishing, and international finance, in dictating world teenage fashions and lifestyles, as well as its diplomatic and military predominance. It is easy to see why intellectuals in France, Islamic clerics in Iran, and any number of Third World dictators should suspect that the Internet is a tool of American cultural imperialism. To many, the freedom, individualism and increasing commercialism of the net seem to indicate not so much an indication of a new world order but the export of characteristically American values to an unwilling world.

Summarizing the likely cultural impact of the Internet and IT in general is a difficult task. In line with a frequent theme within, however, it is worth emphasizing that no outcome of technical change is inevitable or totally predictable. The policy decisions of governments and the ingenuity of groups and individuals may discover undreamed of opportunities latent in current technologies. New technological advances may easily undo the many assumptions behind the preceding discussion.

What is clear is that IT will inevitably change how people all over the world understand reality and create opportunities to change that reality. The more individuals and organizations grasp the nature of the technology and its possibilities, the greater the probability they can influence the direction of change. A modest hope is that increased communication and a greater pooling of information should in the long run make it easier for people, organizations and states to reach, if not a consensus on what should be done, at least informed compromises on how to live together.

IT AND DIVISIONS IN SOCIETY

One aspect of the impact of IT on communities which raises some controversial issues is the extent to which it can be seen as promoting or reducing existing divisions in society. These include economic divisions between rich and poor and social divisions between genders, ethnic groups (e.g. people of different national origins or religion) and races.

An optimistic view of this is that information technology, by definition, promotes communication between people and must therefore help to spread social and international understanding. People who are thousands of miles apart, either literally or socially speaking, can communicate through 'chat' groups, bulletin boards or e-mail; they can obtain information on different ways of life through World Wide Web sites and even experience the 'virtual reality' of other ways of life through interactive programs. More efficient production using IT creates more wealth which can be shared amongst all the groups concerned. It can thus be argued that the technology has a built-in bias in favour of reducing social and economic divisions.

Until recently, most communication using IT has been through the exchange of text unaccompanied by images of the senders, so that it has been possible for dialogues frequently to take place between individuals unaware of the race, national origin, religion or gender of the other participants. Indeed it has been a fairly frequent practice in some contexts for participants to misrepresent their age, sex or other social characteristics and thus to some extent experience the world (or cyberspace at any rate) from a radically different perspective to their own. While such behaviour may or may not be justifiable, it certainly enhances the idea that the web is open to everyone regardless of social background!

This rosy view of technology superseding social divisions must, alas, be seriously modified on further reflection. In particular it should not be assumed without question that the exchange of information must necessarily promote understanding. The proliferation of racist websites and the use of the web to organize extremist political action illustrate the possibilities for the use of the technology to make social divisions worse rather than less significant. As multi-media methods of communication replace text (e.g. videoconferencing rather than bulletin boards), the social anonymity of exchanges may well be severely reduced.

The apparent degree of democratic interaction on the web should not mislead us into thinking that everyone can participate equally in using IT. It has to be understood that access to modern technologies is at present restricted to a relatively small minority of the earth's inhabitants - what sociologists would term an 'elite'.

7

UN Policies

Incorporating Gender into Information and Communication Technology

As information and communication technologies (ICTs) proliferate worldwide, their use and importance increases correspondingly. Likewise, the number of development programs designed to address the gaps between the worlds's information-rich and information-poor and the living conditions of the poor through ICTs has grown tremendously.

Women are a strong focus of these programs, since it is believed that Third World women face double and triple inequalities with regard to ICTs. Access to information and communication technologies for women is more difficult when inequalities of gender, race, caste, nationality, and class are taken into consideration. The December 2003 UN World Summit on the Information Society (WSIS) in Geneva devoted a portion of the conference to our focus: the communication of gender in development ICT.

Under the auspices of the International Telecommunication Union (ITU), the WSIS is the first "cyber summit" to debate the changes brought forth by the use of the Internet and other informational technologies throughout the world.

The description of the forum reads as follows:

The information revolution of the 21st century presents a tremendous opportunity for development. For one, ICT can greatly facilitate the flow, dissemination and appropriation of information and knowledge, irrespective of geographical distance. At the same time, it affords a cost-effective means for organizing and sustaining highly dynamic networks, which are fundamentally demand-driven and allow for their member's interactive exchange and participation. This panel discusses how different media and communication technologies (community radio, TV, telephony, Internet) can contribute to more effective development strategies and looks at their role in voicing people's concerns and allowing more active participation in society-both at the local and at the global level.

Within this vision, communication becomes both process (the means through which realities are created and "information and knowledge" are disseminated and appropriated) and product (i.e., increased development and active voice). Using documents from the Preparatory Committee (PrepCom) for the WSIS we focus specifically on the ways in which gender, communication technology, and development are constructed and connected within these discourses.

Our analysis focuses on policymaking instead of on specific ICT projects to better understand how policy visions structure various ICT projects. We understand development as a multidimensional and relational process that entails many levels and layers of communication. Yet as Naila Kabeer points out, the term development (particularly within the context of international socioeconomic development) is ideologically laden and therefore difficult to contain within a singular definition.

There are three main levels where development communication practices and analysis take place: micro, macro, and global. On the microlevel, development communication is focused more on individual or collective behaviour and often includes particular persuasive campaigns promoting certain programs. On the macrolevel, development communication may include infrastructures and policies within particular nation-state borders around communication systems. There may also be efforts to implement and support more grassroots media systems. On the global level, there is the interest of capitalist expansion of media systems, in addition to more international policies surrounding telecommunications.

At each of these levels there may be concerns that are focused on the technical aspects of communication (equipment, services, etc.), program aspects of communication (setting up and promoting particular programs in underdeveloped economies), and policies about communication flow. However, as Jan Servaes points out, there often is a large gap between the national and international communication policies put forth and the realities of these policies being implemented.

Although we will not address each development level or layer explicitly in our paper, we do want to acknowledge that this field of communication and development is vast, and the literature within this field is often interdisciplinary in scope. In this chapter, we adopt a view of communication as the process through which concepts of gender, information and communication technologies, and development are cocreated, envisioned, implemented, and acted upon.

As the UN and other global organizations attempt to increase the capacities and resources of less developed countries (LDCs) through ICTs, it is worth pausing to ask what values and beliefs about technology, culture, and gender frame these visions and how such frames might affect the evaluation of the usefulness and sustainability of these programs from the perspective of the developer and those to whom the programs are targeted. To explore these questions we turn to the field of communication, particularly to the subfield of development communication. We also draw on the more recent feminist and postdevelopment literature that problematizes the very development communication interventions (often mandated or delivered through government or international development institutions) that originate from outside immediate communities and often overlook barriers specific to women.

In what follows, we first examine some theoretical frameworks for studies of communication, media technology (as ICT), and development to broadly consider the possibilities for constructing and positioning gender within these perspectives. In the second portion of our paper, we apply our analytic framework to an analysis of documents from the Preparatory Committee for the WSIS that served as action plans for the December 2003 Geneva summit.

COMMUNICATION PERSPECTIVES

There are two main paradigms that are often associated with development and communication: modernization and capitalist growth versus dependency and underdevelopment. Modernization theory was supported by cold war ideologies and dominated most international communication research in the 1950s and 1960s. It was deeply rooted in neoliberal economic theory, focusing on efficiency and expansion. In terms of communication models, promoters of growth within Third World countries focused on disseminating information to target audiences in attempts to change behavioral patterns, usually via mass media channels.

This model of communication was often based on a unidirectional flow of information with a focus on transmission and persuasion. Dependency theory became popular in the 1970s as a theoretical attempt to correct the modernist paradigm. This model focused more on the distinctions between peripheral Third World countries and core First World countries, with a larger focus on the geopolitics of communication access and flow. This approach often focused on cultural and media imperialism and the penetration, exploitation, and marginalization of Third World countries.

The dependency model questioned the modernization advocates' claim that media can necessarily serve as agents of change and instead focused on the ways that media can serve as means for cultural domination by First World countries and transnational corporations. Throughout the 1980s, both paradigms persisted as the dominant frameworks in international communication research. More recently a postdependency approach has emerged, which is perceived as a split or a synthesis of the two other paradigms.

In contrast to the modernization and dependency paradigms of development communication, alternative models (which include but are not limited to postdevelopment) are concerned not only with economics but also with emancipation from cultural, political, and psychological dependencies on colonial rule. Emerging out of 1960s and 1970s national and international social movements, these models focus heavily on participation by the communities who were targeted for development projects. No longer was the communication process limited to a one- or two-way model; now it was imagined as a multidimensional and horizontal flow of communication and information.

As Jan Servaes points out, these alternative models of communication and development purported to be interested in the endogenous needs of the particular community, focusing on self-reliance, ecologically sound methods that created structural transformation, and participatory democracy. Within these alternative communication models also emerged a more gendered analysis of development projects and policies. Some feminist communication scholars have called for an exploration of the nature of development discourse and communication activities around women and gender.

In her comparative analysis, Nancy Morris looks metatheoretically at forty-four studies done in the area of communication and development and situates these studies within the broad areas of diffusion of innovations theory (DOI) and the participatory model of development, which emerged, in part, from criticism of the modernist emphasis on diffusion theory. DOI work attempts to influence knowledge, attitudes, and participation first through media campaigns and then through interpersonal contact (i.e., social-service workers and opinion leaders) and relies on quantitative methods to assess the impact of such programs and initiatives.

Participatory models of development communication concern themselves first and foremost with issues of empowerment and thus are more likely to focus on the processes through which less empowered groups become involved in creating and implementing programs that address their articulated community needs. These approaches to power among those traditionally without voice, however, are not without their problems regarding design (who determines the need for voice and how such needs should be met?), implementation (who participates and under what circumstances?) and assessment (how should participation be defined and evaluated? how should the goals of the program be assessed, if at all?).

Morris focuses on results and evaluations in both approaches, noting that the criteria for evaluation in both approaches is highly subjective, that they rely on inconsistent sampling, and that they include insufficient detail for outside objective evaluation of reported results. Morris concludes her review by looking at ways these two approaches may benefit and inform each other; however she does not problematize either of these models or look at how the terms of "development" are constructed. She positions development communication as a fixed reality.

Yet both modernization and dependency models of communication and development have a tendency to be based on Western elitism and are aimed primarily at increasing the power of the ruling groups rather than improving LDCs as a whole. The WSIS is an excellent historical moment to explore how these approaches to development communication continue to manifest themselves, especially as new ICTs are espoused to be beneficial to particular populations (such as women) and developing economies.

Critiquing the abstract foci of development and communication, Renee Houston and Michele Jackson posit a technology-context scheme to consider the ways spaces (contexts) are positioned in ICT and development approaches and initiatives. Their concepts are fairly straightforward: technology is defined in terms of the information or communication tool; context is defined as the space in which the technology is introduced. Space and context define and are defined by the tool; space is made up of the material, including the discursive and symbolic, practices that give meaning to the technology.

Houston and Jackson ask two basic questions of ICT and development approaches, specifically in the area of educational programs: (1) Is the constitution of technology separable from context? and (2) Is the constitution of the context separable from the technology? They separate four approaches based on the degree to which the perspectives isolate ICTs from context and vice versa, or integrate the two.

When technologies are emphasized over context, technology is viewed as constructing and determining human progress, culture, and relations. When context is viewed as separable from technology, the presumption often exists that contexts could and should change, but that ICTs and uses of them do not. For our purposes it is important to note that meanings and uses of technologies are constructed and coordinated in specific spaces, and one cannot be isolated one from the other. Communication technologies may be introduced into spaces that are fluid and dynamic.

These spaces may fluctuate, for instance, between the individual or communal, local or global, more or less developed, and so forth. Technologies themselves are altered and adapted by the people who use them. Meaning is made about who does or does not need to use ICTs and what the consequences of such uses should or ought to be.

Each quadrant in Houston and Jackson's plan recognizes the emphasis placed on technology, context, or both. Yet this scheme also pushes us to pose questions regarding gender. Obviously, such determinations hold importance for women, yet the construction of "gender" as a social category needs to be examined carefully within ICT development policies and programs. The place of women's bodies within the spaces of development is often assumed. Womanhood, understood biologically, has often been the singular unifying category used when discussing "gender" in development terms (often disregarding class, race, sexuality, or national origins).

From this essentialized notion of "woman," Western feminist development approaches also often rely on the notion of inherent inequality between women of First and Third Worlds, securing the position of First World feminists as saviors of their poor Third World sisters. The contributions of feminists of colour and Third World feminists from the past twenty years have helped reconceptualize issues of race, nation, and location in relation to gender and development in significant ways. They have asked the key question, what are the political and epistemological implications of ignoring differences among women?

As Bremy Mendoza observes, "Instead of ignoring differences between women, romanticizing feminist global relationships or assuming 'essential' distinctions between First and Third World women, feminist transnationalists depart and theorize from these differences." Chandra Talpade Mohanty, for example, sought to make the operations of discursive power visible to emphasize what was left out of feminist theorizing-namely, the material complexity, reality, and agency of Third World women's bodies and lives.

Using the Houston and Jackson technology-context scheme outlined, we can begin to question the place of gender within perspectives on ICT development, as evidenced in recent WSIS documents. If we highlight gender as a specific and unique component of context, then we can query the ways spaces are or are not constructed in relation to gender and technology and vice versa. Looking again at the two questions and the various quadrants, we could ask the following:

- Quadrant 1: Determinism

Are ICTs understood apart from the gendered constructions of their use? Here we could ask whether the nongendered "nature" of technology is assumed. What is assumed about gender and technology in development programs driven by digital-divide assumptions? New communication technologies, for example, are separate from any specific context or cultural understandings and practices of gender dominance.

- Quadrant 2: Technology as Change Agent

How are gendered spaces constituted apart from ICTs or development? On whose terms does technology serve as change agent? If, for instance, cultural contexts are assumed to be different but gender within those contexts is often assumed to remain stable, there is a male and female nature to bodies and thus to experiences.

- Quadrant 3: Context as Filter

Does the cultural coding of or meanings for ICTs change over time, and if so, how? Do the gendered uses for ICTs change while the technology itself remains unchanged? In this quadrant, the lens of gender and culture serves as a filter through which we come to understand technology.

- Quadrant 4: Integration

If gender, development, and ICT are mutually socially constructed and dynamic and fluid in use, then how can we work reflexively to challenge our assumptions about each of these constructs? How can we evaluate changes in the substance of a context after the introduction of technology? How can we evaluate the changes in technologies after interactions in specific contexts? Rather than focus on the outcomes of technology, this more integrated perspective focuses on how ICTs are part of larger socio-technical processes that interact with both cultures and technologies and occur in specific contexts.

ANALYSIS

Through highlighting gender in the technology-context model for each quadrant, we can focus specifically on the construction and visibility of gendered development spaces in the implementation of information and communication technologies. In the area of technological determinism (quadrant 1), we can analyze the ways digital-divide arguments-those who have access to and those who do not have access to new technologies-position women in LDCs as always or already in need of ICTs to improve the conditions of their lives.

The idea that technology determines the basis for economic, political, social, and cultural relations is influenced by modernization theory. Technology and gender appear as intrinsic to one's value in the global scene. In the second quadrant, the introduction of a specific technology is implemented across a number of contexts. Yet, the contextual nature of gendered experiences or the experiences of development is not questioned or is assumed to be generalizable across (LDC) contexts.

In many ways, such an approach reifies traditional modernist development models. Where the context serves as the filter for how particular technologies are used and understood (quadrant 3), women in different areas may use ICTs for social, political, or economic means, or a combination of all three. In communication studies literature, such research within this quadrant typically includes ethnographies of technology use. The integration perspective (quadrant 4), recognizes that both technology and context are interdependent. The theoretical underpinnings of this fourth quadrant could include both social constructionist and postdevelopment questions of the very categories of "gender" and "development."

GENDER ICT DEVELOPMENT POLICIES WITHIN THE UN'S WSIS

Our use of the context, technology, and gender model to focus on UN policy documents is important here, because the UN and the WSIS are the primary and most recognized funders (and thus shapers) of worldwide development in the areas of gender and information and communication technologies. As our analysis demonstrates, the overriding emphasis within the documents analyzed is on development through technology. Thus women's empowerment and global equality through access and the necessary infrastructure are presumed.

To frame our analysis, we focus primarily on one of the critical areas of concern that emerged from the United Nations' 1995 Fourth World Conference on Women (FWCW): the inequality in women's access to and participation in media and information technologies. We use the context of the FWCW and the Platform for Action, as well as the WSIS, because these have a common agenda for women's empowerment. Also, these conferences and UN documents have served as "powerful informational and organizational forums for feminists from all over the world."

As noted by Esther Chow, at the FWCW "old issues [such] as women's disproportionate share of world poverty and unequal access to work, education/training, and health care were contextualized anew in view of economic globalization, debt crisis, armed conflicts, democratization, and the new world order." In addition to these old issues, there was also the acknowledgment that over the last decade, a number of advances in information technologies have facilitated global communication networks that transcend national boundaries.

As a result, there was a call to use information and communication technology, in addition to other means, to strengthen women's participation in all levels of decision-making and democratic processes. In the context of globalized life, the use of and access to information and communication technologies becomes a crucial part of social and economic development.

Although there are a number of arguments for and against ICTs, some of the main assertions of how ICTs can benefit women in developing countries include e-governance (having access to government documents, updates, news, and information-such as land registrations), health and education information (e.g., computer information kiosks and training centers with agricultural, medical, and other educational information not readily available from informal sources), and e-commerce and shared-interest business networks (advancing economic interests through access to information not readily available before).

During the third meeting of the Preparatory Committee (PrepCom-3) in Geneva (November 10-14, 2003), gender activists from the WSIS Gender Caucus, the WSIS NGO Gender Strategies Working Group, and the Geneva Committee on the Status of Women successfully worked to include gender in the WSIS Declaration of Principles. Paragraph 12 of the WSIS declaration now reads as follows:

> We affirm that development of ICTs provides enormous opportunities for women, who should be an integral part of, and key actors, in the Information Society. We are committed to ensuring that the Information Society enables women's empowerment and their full participation on the basis of equality in all spheres of society and in all decision-making processes. To this end, we should mainstream a gender equality perspective and use ICTs as a tool to that end.

This statement, while acknowledging that women should be a key component to the new information society, makes several assumptions that need to be addressed. First, the role of information in the advancement of women and of society is unquestioned, as is the type and nature of the information assumed to be more developed than what currently exists or has existed in the traditions of the LDCs and groups targeted by the programs. Second, a "gender equality perspective" (defined by those designing the policy) is presumed to be similar across all spaces and contexts and also equally valued by those involved on either end of designing or receiving such a perspective. Utilizing our gender, context, and technology framework, the statement cited above would fall under technological determinism (quadrant 1).

Examples from planning documents most often fall under this quadrant, as the value of technology, development, and a gendered perspective is assumed across all contexts. Nonetheless, clearly portions of the planning documents address the contexts in which the development programs are to take place. In those places, the emphasis is on the need for more infrastructure and education, where appropriate, to advance the goals of developing sophisticated participants in the more developed information society. As an excerpt from the conclusions to the forty-seventh session of the Commission on the Status of Women urges, governments as well as the UN should include, at appropriate levels of government, ICT education for girls and women in the curricula of all educational levels, from early childhood to tertiary level and in continuing education, to promote and ensure women's full participation in the information society.

Other excerpts from this document urge equal access for women to ICT-based economic activities and management and leadership training to enhance women's capacities for advancement (where technology can serve as change agent-quadrant 2). A distinction is made in this document between programs for women and the "integration of a gender perspective in ICT training programmes," (i.e., one which merely adds gender to an existing male perspective), although the differences otherwise are not indicated.

The promotion of best practices through equality of access, protection, and regulation is emphasized throughout all the preparatory documents analyzed for this chapter (e.g., EU contribution to the draft action plan, the Inter-agency Network on Women and Gender Equality, vision statement from the Commission on the Status of Women). In these statements, individuals are valued as consumers and as citizens with rights to equality and protection from fraud.

The document excerpts here provide more detail about the contexts in which technology can be beneficial for the development of women, yet the gendered experience of the technology and, correspondingly, of development is assumed. Policy statements that assume the context is important and serves as a filter (quadrant 3) attempt to provide a local basis for valuing knowledge systems as well as media content while multiplying the possible discourses for ICTs and development. Although markedly fewer such statements appear in the planning documents, those that exist do attempt to view technology through the cultural perspective of its use.

An excerpt from the conclusions of the Commission on the Status of Women states that the policies and programs implemented should respect the value of different and local languages, and promote and encourage local knowledge systems, as well as locally produced content in media and communications, and support the development of a wide range of ICT-based programmes in local languages, as appropriate, and with content relevant to different groups of women, and build the capacity of girls and women to develop ICT content.

As part of a larger statement about enhancing infrastructure and access to ICTs for women, the session conclusions note that knowledge and technology transfer should occur "on concessional, preferential and favourable terms to the developing countries, as mutually agreed, taking into account the need to protect intellectual property rights and the specific needs of developing countries." It is important to observe, however, that statements privileging local knowledge systems and cultural preferences do not exist in the broader planning documents or in the extracts from the reports concerning the implementation of gender in ICT development processes.

While a lack of specificity is understandable given the broad planning and policy agenda of the WSIS and of the Preparatory Committees, the degree to which a cultural perspective is or is not adopted, may be less so. That local values, knowledge, practices and uses for technologies exist provides one level of perspective, but we can ask to what degree local knowledge is homogeneous. Moreover, is it valued by those in positions to design and implement ICT development projects, and if so, how? Quadrant 4 of our framework addresses these concerns.

Conceivably, ICT, gender and development policies, or projects that integrate ICTs with larger socio-processes (quadrant 4) would privilege material contexts and spaces over technological determinism. By providing a thorough and reflexive examination of the construction of information and communication technologies, development and, especially, gender within the context of policy planning and subsequent projects would not negate the role of larger sociopolitical and ideological systems that structure local understandings but instead examine the dialectical tensions that articulate the local in the global and vice versa.

Although none of the preparatory policy documents we examined contains statements that could be placed in this quadrant, there are several excerpts that deserve further examination. In the Draft Declaration of Principles, a section focused on "cultural identity and linguistic diversity" notes that "the information society is founded on respect for and enjoyment of cultural expression."

ICTs should stimulate cultural diversity and multilingualism and governments should devise active policies to that end. Certainly this focus denotes concern with locally produced meanings for the technology as well as uses for that technology that further such expression. However, this position is then countered by the next section entitled "Ethical Dimensions of the Information Society," which notes shared responsibility and accountability to promote "truth," "justice," "solidarity" and "tolerance," values that, one would assume, are variously understood and interpreted based on one's position (or lack thereof), as the developer or the one to be developed.

The paucity of policy and projects that integrate ICTs with larger social, economic, and political processes should not lead us to abandon the framework as unrealistic or impractical. Rather, we can construct some possibilities for imagining policy that reflects the concerns of the fourth quadrant and the projects that might arise as a consequence of such imaginings. We believe this is a worthwhile endeavor, as none of the policy documents or planning statements works to deconstruct what is meant by gender, technology, or development within these specific areas.

Let us start with gender. Although gender is not defined, we see the appearance of a "gender perspective" alongside development and rights (access, protection) for women. In this manner gender and women mean the same thing, yet, importantly, for policy they are not nor can they be the same. Indeed, for the purposes of policy development, identifying a gender perspective necessarily points toward women as an object for that perspective and away from women to emphasize rights presumably given to men (e.g., access to education, technology, political process). Thus women are equated with a gender perspective that redefines them through human (men's) rights.

Our goal here is not to deny that women deserve rights, of course, but that the process of definition itself both essentializes woman as different while reinscribing them as the same, only as less than men. In this instance, the power of the dominant culture to define identities for women is understood and local knowledge of gendered ways of being is rendered invisible. So how might we as policymakers begin to rethink the ways we define and understand gender?

First, we need to distinguish women from gender or a gendered perspective. Second, we need to look for ways that gender distinctions are practiced and expressed locally in collaboration with those participating in ICT development projects. Finally, we need to be self-reflexive and examine the ways we articulate and structure gender through our power to state policy and conduct research in this area.

With regard to ICTs and development, the foundation for the World Summit is a vision of the "new information society," where "in this society, new technologies, in particular ICTs become an essential tool accessible to all, for the attainment of a more peaceful, prosperous and just world, based upon our common humanity in all its diversity."

Articulated as well within this document is a "commitment to the increased role and responsibility" of more developed nations to spread technologies throughout the world. Here, the idea that more developed nations have the role and responsibility (a commitment) to ensure the spread of ICTs to attain social justice positions, with policymakers as paternal benefactors, entrenches policy efforts firmly within technological determinism (the first quadrant of our model).

This discourse of responsibility leaves little room for consideration of alternative definitions of technology or development that might not privilege a top-down approach. Like those who rethink the construction of a "gender perspective" as discussed above, policymakers working within the fourth quadrant would ask the question, who has constructed and defined the "new information society" and under whose terms are LDCs allowed to join this society? ICTs are often unproblematically positioned as the democratic solution to inequality; once people in LDCs have access to new technologies, equality, justice and democracy will follow.

In this chapter we have sought to address two main issues in the area of gender, ICTs, and development: (1) the communication of gender, technology, and development spaces and contexts through policy, in particular the planning documents created for the 2003 Geneva WSIS and (2) the consequences of such constructions for considering the needs and goals of development programs. We have focused on planning documents for the summit, because we believe that the UN and WSIS play a vital role in how development perspectives and projects are created, interpreted, and assessed.

Our analysis of these documents has revealed a focus on ICTs as a (already understood) tool for empowerment for women. The documents' foci on education in and access to ICT for women presume that such actions will enable women to participate as equals to men in their societies. Yet, as other feminist development theorists and practitioners have pointed out, access to education and technology often has a backlash effect resulting in the further discrimination and abuse of women.

Moreover, the unproblematic focus on ICTs as a tool for the betterment of society has been critiqued by numerous scholars. Throughout the discourse on the new information society imagined by the planners of the Geneva summit, we find a utopian perspective of technology; one that envisions technology as the means to empowerment and equality for women. Beyond these concerns, however, the ways that gender itself is constructed in these documents is troublesome. Gender is presumed to mean of and for women, whereas when men are referred to, it is on their own terms.

The relationship between sexed (woman, man, or otherwise) and gendered (male, female, or otherwise) ways of being or perspectives thereof needs to be explicated. Where local knowledge and languages are called for in a few of the statements in these documents, meanings for gender and technology are nonetheless presumed to be understood. The consequences of such assumptions may be such that ICT development programs are seen as imposed, irrelevant, or, even worse, harmful to indigenous cultures.

Where protection is called for on behalf of those targeted for development, the developer in this context is obviously put in the position of defining and structuring practices for those who are "less developed." In this manner, calls for local knowledge and values are always framed by the experience of exploitation by and through the media and new technologies. Although some degree of protection may be imperative, it is also important to note that alternative frames for experiencing, using, and understanding the ICT's are somewhat limited by protectionist and paternalist stances.

So what can the analysis presented here offer scholars and policymakers working in the area of ICT development and gender? First, we offer a structure for analyzing the ways meanings, contexts, and spaces for gender, ICTs, and development are theorized and constructed. We feel that more attention needs focus on the ways the language of ICT, gender, and development presents a dominant story and frame for understanding who needs development, why, and how.

Arturo Escobar argues that "without examining development as discourse we cannot understand the systematic ways in which the Western developed countries have been able to manage and control, and in many ways, even create the Third World politically, economically, sociologically, and culturally." In our analysis of planning and policy documents for the WSIS convention, the language of progress and modernization continues to shape the ways technology, gender, and development are discussed; this discussion has real material consequences for many people.

Second, gender, development, and ICT are all socially constructed-meaning that even as contexts for understanding gender and development differ, so, too, do the uses and understandings of technology. Too often technology is presumed as a constant when a closer look at ICT development projects reveals that uses and understandings of technology vary with space and time. ICT enthusiasts, scholars, and activists argue that computers and other technologies in and of themselves will not meet the basic needs of women. Rather, the starting point must be the real needs of poor women, especially for appropriate information.

In other words, ICTs should give women access to information-treating information as a commodity in the age of globalization. In their critical perspectives of ICTs, Flis Henwood, Sally Wyatt, Nod Miller, and Peter Senker argue there are a variety of ways to understand the relationships between technological change and social change. Some argue that developing nation-states must be full participants in the new communication technologies. Certainly, increasing women's access to information, resources, and communication technologies does not necessarily ensure participatory or inclusive development. Yet technologies are actively shaped by different social groups and are the outcome of negotiation between individuals, groups, corporations, and institutions, often with differing needs and objectives.

Finally, given the relationships between policy goals and language and project creation, implementation and assessment need to be more closely followed and articulated, particularly with regard to funding imperatives. Some scholars dispute the claim that ICT can fix complex social problems. What must also be explored, they argue, is the systematic way in which governments; regulatory agencies, legal institutions, media industries, multinational corporations, and nongovernmental organizations control technology.

Although we certainly have not addressed the complexities of the larger systems that shape the creation, implementation, and distribution of ICTs, we hope that this chapter stimulates a critical dialogue about their use and assessment for women in spaces targeted for development. Moreover, we hope to complicate visions of the new information society, such as those developed for the Geneva summit through acknowledging, examining, and celebrating the complexities of peoples living within those spaces targeted for development.

8

Empowering Women, Technology and (Feminist) Institutional Changes

In 1998, we wrote a grant to support our desires for educational change at our university. Our teaching experiences indicated that women, especially women of colour, arrive at our working-class urban university lacking basic computer skills, that is, knowledge about how to use a computer and how to run basic word-processing, Web browsing, and e-mail programs.

Laurie Fuller's introductory Web-enhanced women's studies courses often enrolled first-generation women university students, fresh from the urban public school system, with limited knowledge of the use of computers. Erica Meiners' graduate educational theory classes consisted of returning adult students, predominantly women, who entered the university after years outside educational contexts; in addition to anxiety about returning to school, they worried about all the "new" technological skills that courses assumed they possessed.

Fueled by this problem in our everyday context and feeling energetic after participating in a grant-writing seminar at our university, we started research for a proposal to access resources to intervene. Researching and writing this proposal shifted us, as feminist academics and organizers, from our relatively familiar epistemological terrain populated by antiracist feminist theories and praxes and by queer theories and communities to a landscape inhabited by frameworks of liberal multiculturalism, positivism, and a "politically and ideologically neutral" language of educational reform.

We quickly found that literature in the area of the problem of women and minorities in the science pipeline frequently signified what we observed at our institution: women continue to be underrepresented in technology, especially in professions that require computer expertise. In science, math, engineering, and technology (SMET), women learn better in a single-sex environment and where relationships are involved, as in cooperative-learning groups.

Additionally, research frames the absence of people of colour, white women, or both in SMET as an economic problem for the nation-state. We used this discussion of the potential negative consequences for "our" U.S. economic (and military) dominance in our proposal as funding sources often state that based on this rationale, they would fund research to identify strategies to recruit and retain women and minorities in SMET fields. Our library check-out lists shifted from cyberfeminist theories and works by transnational antiracist feminist theorists that question the inherent "good" of technology to government-funded reports, research studies, and texts that used frameworks to construct technology as inherently "good" or "neutral."

Based on the language of the official request for proposals (RFP) of the granting agency we targeted, it was clear that successful proposals originated from a positivistic and a (mythic) politically neutral epistemological terrain. We acquired a vocabulary that worked with this paradigm (empowerment, lifelong learning, assessment and evaluation, curricular transformation, quantitative data gathering) and jettisoned familiar terms that signified discourses of poststructuralism, feminism, or critical (race) theory, and we eliminated language that could be perceived as postmodern (dialogues, discussions of power imbalances between students or subjects and professor or principal investigator, reciprocity) or political (feminist, white supremacy).

This desire to pass with a "neutral ideology" also influenced our visions of educational change, as the RFP clearly stated that projects could not discriminate against anyone. (Note, of course, that this requirement for nondiscrimination comes from the critical work of earlier paradigm changers). Our visions of a (feminist) "women only" project could not be explicitly named or advertised as for "women only," even though the purpose of our study and intervention was to create a single-sex classroom environment for women.

We wrote and animated this neutral paradigm despite our belief that race- and gender-neutral educational change is not feasible, and despite knowing that research has demonstrated "neutrality" is not effective. Margaret Eisenhardt and Elizabeth Finkel found that race- and gender-neutral environments in the sciences are neutral only to the white males who construct that environment. In addition, our varied political work has led us to view "race neutral" as frequently a code word for supporting white supremacy.

Minorities, a term that we would not use in our teaching, academic, or activist writing, immediately became an issue. Our preference, given the connotations of the term minorities-less than (whites) in importance and also less than (whites) in numbers-was people of colour or women of colour, yet the call for proposals (and most of the research data) used the term minorities. (Significantly, the data on the problem of women and minorities in the science pipeline is often represented in ways that separate "women" and "people of colour" into two discrete groups.)

When we gave a draft of our proposal to a friend, a physicist who had received many grants for educational change, he said, "the of colour has to go. Use minorities. They will not know what of colour means." We thought about using "people of colour" but decided that nonconformity with no money was unproductive. We also chose the word empower because of its perceived appeal to the granting agency. Significant work in feminist pedagogy and methodology challenges the notion that researchers can empower subjects and participants or those teachers can empower students. We did not know if this critique of and sensitivity to the term empower was shared by government funding agencies; therefore we chose to use empower and minorities.

We spent months working on this proposal to increase the technological literacy levels of women at an urban working-class university in the Midwest. We did not include our ideas about dismantling (or even questioning the neutrality or the assumed inherent good of) the nation-state or educating women to resist white-supremacist capitalist patriarchy but instead wrote a request for money to help "women and minorities" join in the economy. Fortuitously, the American Association of University Women (AAUW) published a report stating "technology was the new boys' club," and we hooked our grant proposal onto their research findings. We wrote fifteen pages articulating a seamless vision of a (closeted feminist) intervention that we believed would facilitate institutional change.

What are the consequences of writing in this different genre to access institutional resources? Professionals use a variety of social languages many times in one day. Why should the use of terms such as minorities or empower constrain us? Language is not neutral; language shapes ways of thinking about ourselves and the world we inhabit. Using the granting agency's language validates an epistemological framework of multiculturalism that is, at best, problematic, and this has the capacity literally to produce subjects and create realities.

Our original feminist praxis-project, born out of the desire to intervene in a local problem, had morphed to require us to defend language and paradigms we previously critiqued, to promise replicable products (when we did not think curriculum was portable or worked when decontextualized), to prepare and promote workforce development for the nation-state, to advocate "race- and gender-neutral" educational change, and to advertise Lifelong Success through

Computer Expertise. We envisioned the grant with social change as the goal, not the increase and diversification of the labour market; yet to get the money, we wrote and performed the latter.

Our idea was an immature "take the money and run" strategy in which female students would get the skills to enter the labour market and support themselves, and simultaneously they would resist white supremacist capitalist patriarchy. Our project, "Empowering Women for Life-Long Success through Computer Expertise," was funded for four years.

Our proposal focused on creating a course that would give women at our institution the tools to succeed at using technology. Four years later, when we reviewed the data collected and reflected on the project, we recognized that the single-sex course held no interest to students at our institution. Instead, the most useful to the participants, and the most surprising to us, was the creation of a small lab and the employment of students to staff the lab and tutor other students. Given the research on women's successes learning technology in single-sex environments, coupled with our own background and familiarity in women's studies environments, we had not thought (nor did the literature on single-sex education) that the single-sex aspect of the course would be a deterrent.

The brochure we developed to advertise the course had photos of women, used the language-"specifically designed for women" and "targeted for women"-and cited data about the state's need for technology workers. Interviews with women who enrolled in the women-only sections demonstrated that they had selected this class not because it was women only-but because of the technology and the statistics cited on the brochure in relation to job opportunities. Interviews further illustrated that many of the female students in fact thought about not taking the class, and they had to defend to family and friends their reasons for taking a course for women only.

This presented a problem throughout the project and illustrates how heteronormativity affects women's educational trajectories. In addition, this wrinkle caused us to reframe our visions of curricular feminist change. Low enrollment does not mean that students would not benefit from participating in the course; yet women at our institution expressed reluctance to take a women-only course. If no female students enroll, despite creative marketing strategies, the course is not an effective educational intervention, nor is it the "best" environment. In addition, little of the literature that looks at the efficacy of women-only learning environments adequately addresses the ways race and class affect single-sex learning environments.

The multi-racial, working-class population that attends our university calls into question single-sex learning environments that do not take into account race and class. Our proposal suggested that curricular transformation would be the location of change; however, empowerment came not from curricular transformation but from peer tutoring and informal workshops. This unanticipated result highlighted the importance of creating spaces where students can participate as legitimate university community members (for our population, this means in part as paid workers) and learn without the notable presence of a teacher, a class or curriculum.

The grant funded a computer lab with five machines, a telephone, a printer, and peer mentors and lab assistants to assist and teach students technology. The lab is located next to the women's studies office, and sofas and coffee tables furnish a small common area outside the lab. Three Latinas and one returning adult white woman composed the first group of assistants, hired in 2000. They decorated the lab with feminist and justice posters and labeled all the computers with the names of famous women scientists. They used the lab as a site for their own work, socializing, and organizing (usually after working hours).

Their job was to staff the lab and teach other students-help them learn to e-mail, to use spreadsheets, to create Web pages, and so forth. They placed signs across the campus and made business cards that they delivered to classes (first to women's studies classes and faculty and then expanding to others) to let students (and faculty) know that one-on-one help was available. Fifteen women have worked part-time as lab assistants over the past four years: five Latinas, one African American, two Asian Americans, one white women in her early 50s, one recent immigrant from Eastern Europe, and five whites.

The assistants work with a range of technological and often academic problems and a variety of students (from women's studies, psychology, education, business, and other departments): the eighty-year-old woman who audits courses and immediately forgets what she learned at the last tutoring session; students who are recent immigrants and left villages with no electricity; students who have no computer at home, did not use a computer in their high school classes, and need help learning the skills to complete a specific assignment.

The assistants' jobs require that they practice the technological skills they acquire, and they become innovative technological and academic troubleshooters. From observation and interviews, it is clear that lab assistants learned from teaching: they increased their own skill levels, became better able to navigate the university and academic context, improved their writing skills, and increased their confidence levels. Most of the lab assistants are first-generation university students who support themselves (and often their families) with loans, scholarships, and part-time employment-representative of the larger undergraduate population at our university.

Typically, the part-time employment these lab assistants had prior to working in our lab consisted of low-wage service industry jobs. Rose, a twenty-two-year-old Latina, worked as a telemarketer and as a fast-food cashier; while this labour enabled her to support herself and her daughter (with some assistance from her family), the jobs did not enhance her resume, nor did they support or coincide with her academic and professional goals (to work in law enforcement).

The paid employment that women did before working in the lab (waitperson, telemarketer, service sales representative, child-care worker, and fast-food cashier) was feminized nonunion service-sector work. At the lab, the assistants were the experts, they had knowledge and skills that others wanted, and they worked in these "expertise" positions in cross-generational and cross-racial contexts. They spoke of feeling empowered by their skills and their success. They referred to their work as "teaching" or "working in the lab," and this gave them a meaningful campus and employment identity.

The material contexts these women face in their lives, how to support themselves and/or their families on low wages, is a critical factor that shapes their academic trajectory. When roles as "worker" and "student" conflict as is the case for many of our students who swell the ranks of the low-wage service-industry sector, the material realities-paying rent, supplying food, and even covering tuition-surpass paying attention in classes. The lab assistants managed to avoid some of this role conflict.

They worked in the same physical spaces in which they studied, and their identity as "worker" overlapped with their identity as "student." Additionally, they received more than the minimum wage for paid work on campus (and above federal minimum wage). For the lab assistants, their on-campus employment provided a connection to a (feminist) community of learners, and they possessed a physical space they considered their own-the lab, their office, their location at the university. Rose expressed this notion of community and personal space: "It was a home for me.

It was like my office and my place on campus. I could do work there in the downtime. And there was always someone for me to talk with if I needed it. It made me know if I came to the university there was a place for me." The lab also became a site for feminist, queer, and other student organizing. In 2001-2002 a lab assistant was also the organizer of the Gay Lesbian Bisexual Alliance (GLBA) on campus, and another was the organizer of the Feminist Majority Leadership Alliance (FMLA). These student clubs used the lab to create promotional materials for events, to communicate electronically with members of the group, and to do research projects together.

The lab space was routinely full of books, posters, notes about campus and community events, pamphlets, and lab participants (or assistants) homework. The lab assistants created or helped to create posters, Web sites, bulletin boards, and listservs for both groups, which enhanced their technological skills and self-confidence: "I learned skills because we would be talking about doing something, like communicate an issue, the voter registration drive, and the computers were always there. We always know we can ask Laurie for help but we could also figure it out ourselves."

Because of the proximity to the women's studies office and the availability of the sofas outside the lab, it was also a hangout for students. Students would organize meetings or leave messages to connect socially "at the lab": "I always know there will be something happening in the lab. At least one person I know will be there talking about a class or a professor or a good story about somebody. You just get connected."

The success of the lab component to teach students technology is not startling. Meaningful work experience, mentoring, community development, and peer learning aid academic growth and the acquisition of technological skills. Learning or legitimate peripheral participation in communities of practice "is a process that takes place in a participation framework, not in an individuai mind."

Thus, learning happens in communities. There was no formal curriculum, no teacher, and no classroom structure, yet the lab assistants, their peers, and the social communities they were a part of learned technology. The two student groups (FMLA and GLBA) used technology as a tool to organize and create relationships. Students wanted to work together to make Web pages for the FMLA or the GLBA; they used technology as a tool for community building and advancing social and political practices they were invested in.

THE REVOLUTION WILL (NOT) BE FUNDED

As the project concludes, we consider not merely the data we have compiled from this research initiative and the intervention we staged but the more discrete components of the project. What are the consequences of a "take the money and run" strategy for those committed to progressive (often radical) social reform in and outside the academy? How does participation in mainstream discursive and epistemological paradigms shift and constrain us in politically untenable positions? How can we access the resources to fuel progressive social change yet resist the recuperative power of dominant, multifaceted institutions and discourses?

For us, our engagement with this project exemplifies a "women's studies" dilemma; how to work within a system one is trying to change. Women's studies scholarship and activism encounter these tensions in the academy and beyond, and the theme of feminist change erupts as we reflect on the project. What subversions are possible, given Audre Lorde's statement about power? "The master's tools will never dismantle the master's house. They may allow us temporarily to beat him at his own game, but they will never enable us to bring about genuine change" (emphasis added).

While we experience Lorde's analysis, we also move to see feminist praxis as layered-how do we alter the paradigm when it is the very paradigm that makes us visible within the eyes of the nation-state and awards us resources to animate and validate this paradigm? How can modes of resistance be conceived and enacted, from within the master's house?

We began the project because we believed (and still do) students must be given the opportunity to develop computer expertise in their college classes. We started the grant viewing our work as "feminist" educators not merely to assist in the shaping of compliant subjects for this economic order; however, what became clear, quickly, was that the women we wrote the grant for needed employment: not just work that would put money in their pockets but meaningful employment.

Although our academic trajectory to this point had continually positioned us to critique the goals of the nation-state and the economic order, our participation in this project illustrated to us the need to be both critical and to work to create employment opportunities that simultaneously "maintain" it. The feminist geographer and activist Ruth Gilmore, writing against the mass incarceration movement, also argues against static notions of power and resistance (working from the writings of Audre Lorde): "One works with what is at hand; the problem is not the 'master's tools' but the effective control of those 'tools.'"

While Gilmore's caution is important, and one of our "tools," language, is clearly not inherently oppressive, contexts can and do control and affix meanings to language that limit, for example, justice initiatives. Yet, in the messy work of praxis, perhaps tools can be temporarily reformed or a different use for the old tools can be forged? Empowering minority women can be a success story of technological skills acquisition and agency and simultaneously a tale of the reproduction of (low-wage) technology workers for the nation-state. Perhaps this doubled move is a kind of tactical resistance? Or, this is the story we tell ourselves at the end of the day. Our advice to (sister) activists is-proceed with caution.

There is no neat and happy ending. Our project, "Empowering Women for Life-Long Success through Computer Expertise," did enable female students who completed the course to attain a higher level of confidence and technological abilities. The meaningful (and paid) apprenticeship of the lab assistants during the same period enabled them to acquire a wider range of skills and, most important, a kind of technological fluency.

Although acquiring the resources to support this change was significant, negotiating how language and epistemological frameworks shape and constrain projects and political action also has been a valuable "finding." We end the project with the knowledge that we were naive to hope to "take the money and run," yet the process enabled us to gain perspective on the importance of implementing (and theorizing) educational and institutional change.

BLACK WOMEN, TECHNOLOGY, AND IDENTITY

Race and gender take on a number of different forms when they intersect with technology, although most of those permutations resemble their "real time" counterparts, where atavistic attitudes and practices exist alongside progressive views and activities. This chapter engages the topic through three different venues: the current discourse on race and technology (the digital divide), the experiences of black women who work in technology, and the figuration of race and gender on the Web. The overarching question that links these three different sections is whether black women can find a "room of their own," as it were, in cyberspace.

As Lisa Nakamura argues in *Cybertypes: Race, Ethnicity, and Identity on the Internet*, the myth of cyberspace as a "raceless, genderless and sexuality-free" space is one that thrives in a variety of chat room and other on-line forums. Nakamura argues that "race is constructed as a matter of aesthetics, or finding the colour that you like, rather than as a matter of ethnic identity or shared cultural referents. The fantasy of skin colour divorced from politics, oppression or racism seems to also celebrate it as infinitely changeable, customizable; as entirely elective as well as political".

All of these identities, of course, exist in and are constantly reconstructed through language, a medium that, even in the age of Java, still rules as the central means of signification on the Web. Indeed, the success of one's Web site, career, or product can often rest almost entirely on words-that is, whether they possess that magic combination that will earn them a spot in the top ten of a Google search. It also goes without saying that the language used in cyberspace operates in much the same way it does in the "real world."

In the Western imagination, technology is the exclusive provenance of the West-it is by default always white, almost always male, and sexuality rarely emerges as an imaginative category. The reality is that technology is the product of ten thousand years of world civilizations, of which African civilizations were a central contributor, and African Americans have been regular contributors, from ironing boards to cell phones. The reality of the digital divide.

An August study from the University of California, Los Angeles had the former in the top spot by tallying the number of times each minority group used the Internet per month. Articles that focus on the total amount in computer sales put blacks ahead of Latinos and whites, in that order, but note that Asian Americans are far ahead of everyone else (a fact rarely mentioned in other articles). These articles appeared in 2000 and 2001, so it is unclear if this is still true. Yet another article dated January 23, 2004, on BET.com noted that African Americans still lag woefully behind whites in Internet use and access (no other racial groups are mentioned).

It must be noted, though, that the author argues that blacks comprise 13 percent of the population and yet make up only 8 percent of Internet users; point taken, but most estimates of the percentage of blacks in the total American population cite a range between 9 percent and 13 percent, so the lag depends on which end of the scale one chooses to cite. There are, of course, many ways to gauge Internet use. Most interesting were the findings of the Pew Internet and American Life Project, which examined the purposes members of different racial groups had for the Internet; in 2000, researchers found that 45 percent of African Americans, compared to 35 percent of whites (no other racial groups were mentioned), used the Internet for information on health care.

African Americans were also more likely to use the Internet to look for information on jobs, housing, religion, and hobbies, whereas whites were more likely to use the Internet to stay in touch with friends and family. Two years later, the same research group found that African Americans were twice as likely as whites to use the Internet for career networking, and Latinos were one and one-half times more likely to use it for this purpose than were whites.

One point on which all of these studies agree is that the number of African American Internet and computer users has grown by leaps and bounds in the past few years, and most studies note that this jump coincides with the rapid decrease in hardware prices. The arguments proposed by scholars such as Anthony Walton and Henry Louis Gates, Jr., that the digital divide is not primarily economic but racial (Gates pointed to lack of initiative on the part of the African American working class, and Walton argued that technology has been the historical enemy of African Americans) now strike us as, at best, simply wrong, and at worst racist in their logic. The barrier, it seems, as it is so often, has less to do with race than with money.

Virginia, who is a generation older than Eileen, began by studying business at a prestigious state university, but after working in administration for a few years during the late 1960s and early 1970s, realized she was not in a lucrative career path. She returned to school while working and began to take computer courses, because she found them interesting. One of her mentors at work suggested she take a computer aptitude test, and her high scores convinced her she should switch to IT as a career. From about 1975 to 1985, Virginia worked in program design and moved into code programming.

Like Virginia, Jill and Eileen had originally planned to major in business administration to create a foundation for future careers but became interested in pursuing careers in technology after taking some courses in computer programming. Technology, Jill and Eileen said, appealed to them because it was innovative and constantly changing. While the marketability of technology skills informed their career decision, it was the excitement of participating in an industry that opened so many new intellectual possibilities and skill challenges that initially drew them.

Jill and Eileen moved to the Twin Cities several years ago after receiving job offers from the same multinational corporation that was seeking to upgrade its systems. Jill, Eileen, and Virginia now work as senior systems analysts, and Eileen does extensive volunteer work through a national nonprofit organization run by African American technology professionals committed to making computers and technology more accessible to African American communities across the United States. When I asked about the roles race and gender play in their careers, both noted that they saw the number of local African Americans in their field (already less than 1 percent in their own company) starting to decline even further.

At the same time, they noted that, in their experience, the decline in minority personnel was due to several factors: the economic slump, a general trend of African American white collar workers seeking careers outside the Twin Cities, and, according to Jill and Virginia, racist practices by management (Eileen said she has not personally witnessed racist treatment). With a career that will soon span three decades, Virginia elaborated the most on the racist and sexist practices she has witnessed in three different jobs, ranging from insulting comments to having work that had been allocated to her based on her skills given to white junior colleagues who had yet to acquire comparable skills and experience.

When asked her if she thought there was an implicit racial and gender hierarchy in terms of promotion, recognition, and treatment, Virginia said that in the thirty years she has worked in the field, every company she has worked at had the same race and gender hierarchy: white men were fast-tracked to top salaries and positions, followed by white women and then black men, with black women at the bottom. I cut in at this point to comment about how statistics showed that in the past twenty years black women were receiving bachelor's, master's and doctoral degrees at rates much higher than their black male counterparts, but that those numbers dropped significantly behind black men when it came to finding employment that reflected their advanced degrees.

Virginia replied that her own work experiences reflected those statistics, in that she knew of many black women who were rejected in favor of their white and black male counterparts despite having comparable or even more advanced training. "We [black women] have the education but we don't have the power," she noted. When I asked Jill and Eileen about their perceptions of and experiences with the digital divide in their own lives, the local black community, and nationwide, both expressed very similar opinions. Neither saw a striking degree of computer illiteracy in their local communities, nor did they have a sense that there was a dramatic difference between whites and blacks beyond local communities.

While this did not mean, in their view, that African Americans enjoyed the same access to computers and the Internet as white Americans, it did mean there were other factors that were as or more important than race when it came to ease of access and technological familiarity, with age and income topping the list. Virginia agreed with this assessment, but added that she had observed African Americans receiving inferior treatment at national chains that sell and repair hardware, software, and peripherals, leading her to conclude that while, in her experience, blacks and whites both lacked the necessary depth and breadth to recognize and then address problems they themselves could fix, the former suffer the most for this lack of knowledge, in treatment and in the higher amounts they are charged for repairs.

Eileen talked more extensively about her views on and experiences with technology access and education in the black community, as she devotes quite a bit of her time as a volunteer teaching African American high school students (grades 9 through 11) computer programming (for example, building Web sites) and proper use of the Internet as an information resource. In her experience, different sectors of the black community face different challenges: for example, senior citizens need easy physical access and training that would familiarize them with computers and the Internet, while students need longer access hours (a requirement not met by the limited usage offered by their public schools and libraries) that are also affordable; for the latter, this would mean, in most cases, free access.

Eileen pointed out that the black students she works with are especially enthusiastic about learning computer programming and Internet use, taking what they have learned from her to do further research on the Web, so that, by the next class, they have jumped ahead by several steps. "I have to work that much harder just to keep up with them!" she laughed. Jill, Eileen, and Virginia agreed that lack of resources, not enthusiasm or curiosity, promoted computer illiteracy-a situation, they pointed out, that was not race-specific but rather endemic to any community that is economically challenged or possesses members who grew up long before the computer revolution.

In other words, rather than reading the World Wide Web as a medium that mainly produces distorted views of African Americans and African American women, they felt the Web offered counter-discourses that subverted the racist and sexist discourses they found all across the local and national print and television media. Virginia differed slightly in this assessment, as she rarely surfs the Web anymore.

The increase in African Americans on the Internet is reflected on the Web. Four years ago, all the major Web sites (that is, those regularly maintained and run by organizations as opposed to personal Web pages or sites that were not updated at least yearly) by and about black communities in North America, the Caribbean, and western Europe; nowadays. The proliferation of Web sites by and about African Americans alone ranges from academic studies to community organizing, to hobbies, to professional societies (the majority of which, unsurprisingly, are devoted to African Americans who work in IT). The most common sites, to name just a few, are javanoir.net, Afamnet.com, everythingblack.com, sistahspace.com, new.blackvoices.com, bdpa.org, and africast.com.

Yet the proliferation of Web sites by and about black communities in the West has also brought into focus the ways in which Web spaces specifically designated for peoples of African descent practice their own types of discrimination, and in fact can reflect the same types of prejudicial assumptions and exclusions that dominant groups are prone to practice both on the Internet and in the quotidian. Because, as Nakamura and others have pointed out, the ways in which race operates on the Web reflect our attitudes when we log off, I want to offer a bit of background on the relationship between belonging and space that presaged the invention of the Internet and affects it.

It is unfortunately a truism that the question of belonging-that is, the intersection between identity and one's home space-is far from resolved in African American communities, and much of the tension centers on the same issues one finds in all American communities: homophobia, xenophobia, sexism, and misogyny. While the Black Nationalist movements of the 1960s and 1970s did much to uplift the socioeconomic conditions of some black communities and did even more for African Americans' self-empowerment, it also further valorized chauvinist, heteropatriarchal assumptions about the nature of black identity.

In short, despite the impressive role of the movement's leaders and organizers in abolitionist, antilynching, education, and voting rights movements, the marginalization of black women that started during the civil rights movement still continues today, both in discourse and practice. While many academics (including myself) understand Black Nationalism as having come to an end in the late 1970s, it is more accurate to say that those structures created in the late 1950s and 1960s no longer exist in their original form.

The original intent and spirit of Black Nationalism is still very much alive and well, and that is not all good, especially for black women and those who disagree with or otherwise fail to conform to the heteropatriarchal ideologies that still gird those structures. Any discussion about blacks and belonging in the West must engage with Black Nationalism. Almost since the moment blacks first arrived on North American shores, some form of Black Nationalism has been propagated and disseminated among the black communities in North America, the Caribbean, and Europe. This makes sense: originally a relatively disparate group of people from different nations with radically different histories, the Ibo, Ife, Yoruba, Fante, and other West African nationalities were recategorized as "Negro" by Western philosophers and scientists, and simultaneously defined as subhuman and in need of reeducation-that is, slavery.

Even so, from the outset, these diverse groups rapidly made common cause with one another as a means of support and resistance. Dispersed across several thousand miles of land and water, black writers such as David Walker and, later, W. E. B. Du Bois, and Marcus Garvey envisioned and advocated a "black nation" that, while without the legitimizing force of a formal state apparatus (government, laws, geographical borders), was nonetheless united by a common belief in the right of self-determination for all peoples of African descent in the West.

Except, most often, for women. In deliberately drawing upon Enlightenment discourses on the nation by figures such as Ernest Renan, David Hume, and G. W. F. Hegel, black male thinkers in the diaspora sought to underscore the hypocrisy of a civilization that claimed to have achieved the highest form of sociopolitical organization, human suffrage and equal rights, and yet was intensely mired in the ghastly business of capturing, selling, brutalizing, killing, raping, and exploiting other human beings. With the exception of W. E. B. Du Bois, all of the black male writers on the black nation failed to consider black women as human beings worth mentioning, except as the humiliated symbols of white male lust and black male disempowerment.

In the past 350 years, very little has changed, and the political logic of black nationalism, in both black communities and black studies, has undergone very few permutations, especially with regard to the role of women-not to mention sexual minorities. As Madhu Dubey and Deborah Gray-White have noted, a rather striking low point was reached in the 1970s, when the argument that empowered black women were an unacceptable threat to black men was earnestly put forth both by the Black Panthers and conservative Democrat Daniel Patrick Moynihan.

Dubey writes, "Appropriating Moynihan's matriarchy thesis, these black nationalists seemed unaware that the government's production of a discourse that highlighted black men's lack of masculine privilege in the family served to displace and disguise their economic oppression in the labour market. The matriarchy myth effectively split the racial discourse of black nationalism along gender lines, aligning black men with white men in their common commitment to a patriarchal family system."

For most heterosexual black men, then, and for some black women, this question of belonging was settled, as it were, by black nationalism; the vast majority of academic and laymen's books that continue to question and explore (as opposed to assert) issues of black identity and belonging in the West are in fact books written by and about black feminists and queer rights activists such as Patricia Hill Collins, Audre Lorde, Philip Brian Harper, Hazel Carby, Michele Wallace, Angela Davis, and Roderick Ferguson (just to name a few).

They often begin, unsurprisingly, with a critique of Western nationalism and Black Nationalism. Despite the proliferation of these discourses that remind us that all forms of nationalism rely upon the designation of one group as outsider/Other to the nation (with this Other most commonly being women, but frequently cast as nonwhite or nonheteronormative), African American communities on the local and national scales remain as wary of, dismissive of, and as hostile to black women's empowerment as their nonblack counterparts.

DIASPORA AND TECHNOLOGY

So where do black women find their place? If we look first at the United States, we see some answers: over the past twenty years, the number of African American women attending colleges or universities has increased 400 percent, and these numbers hold true for both historically black colleges and universities and what are known as "Black/White Institutions" (for example, Notre Dame, Amherst, Yale,

UCLA). And, whether they move into business, medicine, academe, nonprofits, or any other profession, these women are receiving the same education in information technology as their nonblack counterparts.

Nonetheless, spaces have been created and "updated," as it were, in the drive to offer a counter-discourse to black identity and belonging that does not rely upon heteropatriarchal and heteronormative exclusions; it goes by many different names or at times goes unnamed, but call it "diasporic discourse." Beginning with black feminist and queer activists in the 1970s, such as Audre Lorde and Barbara Smith, the concept of the African diaspora as a space that is neither created nor maintained by the heteronormative remains strong.

These academics and activists encourage us to both understand and define the African diaspora as a fluid, heterogeneous collective that operates through fluid, elective affinities, defying the established heteropatriarchal norm Black Nationalism seeks to impose on diaspora studies. Quite obviously, this is not as easy as it sounds. Some proponents of diaspora have argued that the term cannot be invoked unless one engages with and speaks to all communities in the African diaspora-if one excludes Africa from consideration, these scholars would still require us to invoke and learn almost every single western and eastern European language (there are black communities in nearly all of them), as well as the various dialectics that operate in the Caribbean and South America.

As no scholar has come forward with this bounty of talents, the logic of this argument would dictate that we maintain our silence until one emerges. Yet this position nonetheless raises an important question: how indeed does one speak of diaspora without making certain elisions? We can see one practical reason Black Nationalism remains so attractive: in addition to offering the mostly reassuring veil of homogeneity (except when one feels oneself forced to conform, of course), it also allows an elegant simplicity of rhetoric and thought that attracts both the academic and the layperson.

Nationalist assumptions often operate in two distinct ways: the abilities and parity of other similar groups are ignored, or the nation situates itself as wholly delineated from these groups either explicitly or implicitly. In other words, the idea of "different and equal" simply does not operate. In Web sites featuring black achievements and timelines of important events, black men dominate the pages. Whether it is in the lists of historical achievements, artistic and literary creations, sociopolitical movements, or technological discoveries, most black women who have been and continue to be significant contributors are mentioned with far less frequency.

The rhetoric is also telling: in the majority of Web sites that detail these achievements, "black" means "African American," effectively erasing the contributions of men and women of colour in the West who are black Britons, black Caribbeans, black French, Afro-German, etc. While there are contexts in which this interchange between two very different terms is acceptable, lists titled "Black Inventors" or "Famous Moments in Black History" inevitably suggest that only African Americans have made an impact and contributed to Western civilization. In the Web sites I listed above, the focus is almost exclusively on African Americans although the themes and topics listed, such as racism, current news, and global trends in the economy, are created by and speak to a wide range of peoples of African descent across the globe.

Yet what better space than cyberspace to imagine diaspora? With its emphasis on hyperinclusion, fluidity, and the need for understanding alliances as a series of intersections rather than coercive categories, with the Internet's ability to hyperlink and thus offer every text as a set of intersections, the black feminist and queer mandate mentioned earlier can in fact be realized. This has already been noticed. Sistahspace.com is one such Web site. When one first searches for "Sistahspace," a list of Web sites from around the world is summoned.

Black women can find a "space" here, then, albeit not necessarily the kind that all who visit it would expect. This space is not clearly delineated or discretely bounded; it is, rather, a point of several intersections leading to other sites of connection, some of which we will find reassuring and familiar, others that we will find unfamiliar, possibly hostile. Such is the logic of diaspora, however, where difference must be negotiated rather than manipulated to reflect what we want.

Those scholars who advocate understanding the African diaspora as a counterpoint to the exclusionary organizing logic of nationalism struggle to replicate this fluidity on the two-dimensional page (which, as Jacques Derrida glumly noted in On Grammatology, is depressingly unilinear). We need to engage with the Internet beyond Web surfing and checking e-mail. In not engaging with technology in our exploration of diaspora, we make the same mistake of which we accuse others, namely, determining the technological as a discretely bounded, clearly delineated space that belongs to computer nerds rather than to "serious" scholars.

By "respecting" the supposed integrity of this space, we close ourselves off from the millions of Internet users of all nationalities, genders, races, and sexualities who are far less likely to read the books, journals, and articles we write and edit, but who nonetheless are curious about the very topics we study and write about. If we do not add our voice, we allow this space to remain largely heteropatriarchal, with Web sites such as Sistahspace.com remaining the exception rather than the rule.

Those of us who believe our work can and should speak to audiences beyond the ivory tower need to engage the Internet as a discursive space not only because it can help us explore the dizzying chronotopic demands of diaspora, but because it is increasingly the site where those ideas and ideologies that Nakamura so eloquently outlined function ever more frequently and broadly.

GIRLS AND TECHNOLOGY CAREERS

If you ask most children to draw a picture of a computer scientist, you will probably get a picture of a man in a lab coat working in a cubicle. The images in these drawings reflect a problem with the way today's youth perceive technical careers. Most students do not imagine a career in the field, and for girls, a career in technology is especially unlikely. When they do study technology, girls are more likely than boys to work on clerical skills, in courses that do not prepare them for careers in advanced technology fields. Even girls with positive experiences with computers are not inclined to study more advanced technologies.

We talked with girls in our community to find out what kinds of technology projects appealed to them and used the findings to design a program for girls. The resulting program, Techbridge, is sponsored by Chabot Space and Science Center in Oakland, California. Techbridge introduces about 250 girls annually to a variety of applications of technology that include digital storytelling, building robots, programming, animation, and career exploration.

The after-school technology programs are hosted at elementary, middle, and public high schools in Oakland and surrounding communities and at the California School for the Blind in Fremont. The primary sources of data for this chapter are in-depth interviews and focus groups with 126 Techbridge girls and 34 of their parents or guardians. The girls ranged in age from eleven to nineteen years old, with most in the twelve- to fifteen-year-old range. We selected girls who had a broad range of involvement and skill levels within their programs and who reflected the range of racial and socioeconomic backgrounds in their schools.

Forty-two girls are African American, twenty-six are Asian, twenty-nine are white, twenty-one are Hispanic, and eight are multiracial or other. Interviews were conducted in English, Cantonese, or Spanish and were structured around a set of open-ended questions. Data were analyzed using a grounded theory method, as developed by Anselm Strauss and others.

The goals of Techbridge were to engage girls in learning and using technology, to embolden their plans for further study in technology, and to increase their interest in pursuing careers in technology. Although adolescents may be several years away from entering the workforce, information about their plans for their future gives an indication of their intentions to pursue classes and extracurricular opportunities that increase their chances of an academic and career path in technology. To explore these issues, we asked girls the following questions about their career interests and future plans: What do you want to be when you grow up? What kinds of classes do you need to prepare for your career choice? Where do you think you will be in ten years? What do you have to do to get there?

We were surprised to find that even with positive experiences in the program; most girls did not aspire to careers in technology. One girl told us, "I like computers a lot," and "Everything that we've been doing so far [in Techbridge] has been fun." Yet, when asked about her career goals, this student explained, "It seems like I'm interested in technology, not as a career, but as a habit." In a focus group, four middle-school girls described the technology in Techbridge as "fun, so amazing, interesting, makes me feel smart." But minutes later, these same girls closed the door to career options in technology, saying, "I don't plan on doing it as a career," and "I like it but it's not something I would grow up to do." In exploring why some girls did not see technology as compatible with their interests and identities, we discovered that girls face a number of hurdles in the educational pipeline for technology careers.

Girls told us that even though they enjoyed working on computers in Techbridge, they would not want jobs where they "look at a computer screen all day" and "come home with headaches." Many girls believe that it might be boring to work with computers and be confined to an office: "I would really hate to be stuck at the computer all day.... I would rather have a job that's more involved with the world." With images of "little cubicles and people sitting glued to the computer," it is understandable that some students do not aspire to technology careers.

After hearing descriptions like these, we asked the girls to describe their images of persons working in technology fields. One group of middle-school girls, adamantly not interested in technology careers, offered the following description: "They look hecka smart because they are wearing those little glasses... and lab coats... probably geeky and use vocabulary that you wouldn't understand and be able to keep up with." When asked about the gender and race of these workers, this group of African American girls agreed that they imagine men who are white or Asian.

These stereotypes did not lessen with age, as high school students expressed the same impressions. One high-school student described technology workers as "smart.... They've got to be kind of nerdy," and added, "I'm not that type of person.... They don't do anything. They don't talk on the telephone... they don't want to do anything but study... it's not a good life." Her description paints a picture of an antisocial person, who is single minded in his or her focus on work. By distancing herself from "that type of person," this student is creating a barrier between herself and people who have careers in technology.

Not all girls in Techbridge were reluctant to consider a career in a technical or scientific area. Some discussed their plans to become a Web designer, graphic artist, or computer technician. Although hearing these goals is inspiring to anyone interested in increasing girls' advancement in these occupations, we found an alarming disconnect between the stated dreams of many of these girls and their plans to achieve their goals.

Many of the girls who expressed interest in technical careers had little information about what the jobs entailed. For example, when asked which type of technology career she was interested in, a high-school girl said, "I've thought about that real hard. I don't know what kind of technologies there are out there." Presently, this student enjoys working on projects in Techbridge. However, without knowing about specific career options in technology or being acquainted with anyone who could serve as a role model, it may be hard for the girl to maintain her interest in the field.

In addition to lacking information about careers in technical fields, many students were uninformed about how to prepare for their career goals or the demands the process entails. For example, a middle-school student told us she was interested in pursuing a career in engineering, but when asked if she knew what courses in high school she would need to prepare for a college major in engineering, she admitted, "No, not really." Because engineering programs in college typically have prerequisites of advanced high-school math classes, a lack of knowledge about these entrance requirements can effectively obstruct her entrance into the major. One girl wanted to be a pediatrician, yet she had no plans to take advanced science classes. When students were asked follow-up questions about the future, they demonstrated a lack of basic knowledge about courses needed to stay in the pipeline for their chosen careers.

In many cases, students reported more than one career interest. Frequently, the two careers would represent highly distinct areas of study. First was "dream" careers-like singer, actress, or basketball player-that often embodied fame and fortune in popular media. The "back-up" careers included computer programmer, pediatrician, or attorney. For example, a sophomore was interested in a career in singing or dancing and veterinary science. She told the interviewer that she needed to go to college to "get an education," but when asked what she was planning to study, she answered, "What I'll study in college is actually performing arts."

The back-up careers were often afterthoughts, and most girls we interviewed demonstrated no awareness that these career choices would require years of education. Nor were the students taking any concrete steps toward those goals, such as taking advanced math or science classes or looking for internships to prepare for these careers. As discussions unfolded, it became evident that they were unlikely to attain the back-up careers. Some girls said they anticipated difficulty persevering through challenges and doing the hard work required to achieve long-term goals. A seventh grader who expressed interest in becoming a doctor to "find cures for things" acknowledged, "But I may change my mind because it takes a long time and I'm not willing to wait that long." Another student, who aspires to be a doctor, initially said that in ten years "Probably I'll be in school." However, in her next sentence, she retracted, "Not really, because I don't like school."

For these girls, career choices involving professional and technical careers appear to be more important as objects of discourse than as paths the girls actually plan to follow. Unless they receive career guidance and understand the benefits an advanced educational degree can bring, these students will face enormous challenges and difficulties achieving their dreams of careers that require years of challenging studies and professional training.

To understand how girls develop beliefs about careers and plans to attain their goals, we studied the kinds of career guidance and support that parents provide. We asked whether the ethnic backgrounds and socioeconomic status of families affect the pattern of guidance and support that girls receive. We found great variation in how parents shape and support their daughters' career aspirations. Some parents are extremely involved and supportive, while others are primarily hands off. Minimal Career Guidance from Parents: Many of the girls we interviewed reported receiving little or no career guidance from home. When asked the question, what does your family hope you will do when you grow up? Most girls told their parents said little and would support whatever careers the girls wanted to pursue. The following comment from a middle-school girl typifies the laissez-faire attitude of parents: "They just want me to do what I like to do. They go along with what I like."

Asked about advice they receive, the majority of girls said the most direction they receive is to graduate from high school and attend college. In families where parents had not attended college, this message was especially strong. An African American ninth grader described her mother's interest in her attending college: "She wants me to go because nobody in my family's ever gotten a college degree. She always tries to sign me up for stuff that has to do with colleges." Beyond advising their daughters to go to college, most parents provided no further direction. A Hispanic high-school student told us, "They don't really know what I should study. They haven't told me anything about it, so I guess it's up to me to know what I want to do." Some girls expressed discomfort with the responsibility of having to make all the decisions on their own and to do so without guidance. A high-school girl explained that greater direction beyond "just graduate" from parents would be helpful: "I think if the family sits down and talks about things that could help in your lifetime [that] will make you think and start planning. I think it would mean a lot coming from parents."

The Consequences of an "Open Attitude" toward Careers: Many parents said they are reluctant to be directive with their daughters' academic and career paths. They maintain "open" attitudes to different areas of study and do not encourage their daughters to focus on one career in middle and high school. Rather, these parents encourage their daughters to try many different activities. One mother told us, "I would like to open doors for her to all kinds of things, so that when she wants to make a decision on her own, she has more choices." Several parents shared the belief that their daughters may do many different jobs throughout their lives and that a broad education is the best way to meet these demands. One mother explained, "It's really important to be flexible and not too narrow early on in their interests and in their education."

Interventions to support girls' growing interest in science and technology need not be regarded as controlling or limiting girls' choices but rather as offering opportunities to "test the waters" and gain experiences that will help students in whatever career paths they eventually take. Girls' current career interests could be encouraged and supported through field trips, extracurricular activities, and internships. By not providing early support for specific career interests, parents may unintentionally exclude some professions that require considerable advanced planning and training. Parents' reluctance to support specific career choices may unknowingly hinder their daughters' ability to stay on a technical or scientific educational and career path. We looked at the kinds of support and expectations that girls from different racial and socioeconomic groups received.

When a group of white parents was asked how their daughters joined Techbridge, they described limited involvement and believed this to be common for all parents of adolescents. One mother noted, "I think when you have a sophomore in high school, they're increasingly autonomous. You get a form to sign and that's about it. Once in a while, I'll get glimpses of what's truly going on in [my daughter's] life."

The limited influence these parents take for granted was challenged by African American, Asian, and Hispanic parents. Although some parents may not speak English, and therefore must rely on their children to translate information about school activities, we found that they nevertheless provide important support and direction. When describing which high-school academy to select, one Asian girl from a first-generation immigrant family stated, "I couldn't make up my mind whether I would go into health or engineering. And my dad finally decided, 'You should go into engineering.' So he decided that for me."

Similarly, an African American father repeatedly described making academic decisions for his fifteen-year-old daughter. When he decided that she should be in the Engineering Academy, he described the process as simply, "I said, 'This is the way it's going to be.'" His daughter's wishes apparently never entered into the conversation and were not discussed as part of the decision-making process. In contrast, when one white girl described her decision not to join the Engineering Academy because she does not like math, she noted only in passing, "Well, my mom had kind of wanted me to [join the Engineering Academy]." This mother did not have the strong influence exercised by other parents.

Some parents provide career guidance with the hope of helping their children use education as "a way out" of economic hardship. These parents engage in career counseling more actively. One African American mother of a middle-school girl put it this way:

> I just know for African Americans, education is one of those things that we see as a way out.... I think for a lot of people of colour, we just realize that the only way to participate in society is by finding some sort of career to step out. So I think in our homes, maybe even a little bit more, we're talking about that.

Although this mother recognizes the importance of race in her active encouragement of her child, the theme is repeated across other ethnic groups in families with lower educational backgrounds and lower-paying jobs. A white mother who did not complete college reported, "Neither of [my parents] counseled me. They never said, 'You have to get a job when you grow up....' And I never knew what my options were. So I talk about it." In contrast, in families with higher socioeconomic levels, career counseling was often not an important discussion topic. During a focus group with five white, highly educated, upper middle-class parents, we asked what kind of career guidance they provide their high-school daughters. The mother of a tenth grader said, "As far as career counseling and those sorts of things, that is light-years away from where my daughter is right now.... These are not discussions which she and I have."

These parents assume that their daughters will attend college and achieve satisfying careers. However, they may not realize that unless they actively encourage their daughters' interest and engagement in technical fields, the young women may find some doors already closed. For example, engineering attracts students with a targeted career focus in high school, and many engineering programs require that students declare a major as a freshman.

While most parents we spoke with did not actively steer their daughters toward technical careers, a few families in our study did take a strong position in supporting their daughters' interest in these fields. In these families, parents, siblings, or other close relatives have extremely rewarding technical careers. The guidance and support provided in these families are multifaceted and substantial; parents engage their daughters in conversations and activities that provided in-depth information about the career field, often talk about their work, and convey their emotional satisfaction with their job. A first-generation Asian immigrant mother who uses computer programs at work described her daughter's interest in computers:

> She wants to do everything I do. I think mostly because I enjoy my job. And when I learned HTML, she learned it. And she wants to be a programmer when I talk about it.... I share the things that I like with her, and then she gets excited and she wants to learn too.

This same positive influence from a parent's career was evident when a white middle-school girl described the influence and involvement of her mother, who is a scientist: "She'd tell me about these things and I'd be fascinated and we'd go into her work and look at the machines. So very early on I got interested in science because that's all that was talked about." Like the previous student, this girl also expressed interest in a scientific and technical career. Her perceptions of careers in science and technology were quite detailed and positive, as were her images of persons working in these fields: "I've met a lot of them and they are really nice people and they seem to be a lot more interesting than normal people."

A high-school girl whose family recently emigrated from India described a relative who is a computer programmer as the source of her interest in a technology career: "My uncle really inspired me because I saw that although you probably have to work a lot, you are doing what you like." This girl has a positive image of those who work in technology and, interestingly, explained her interest with some of the same traits like "working hard" and "sitting at the computer" that other girls used as reasons for why they would not want to pursue a technical career. She also talked about the guidance and the expectations of her parents and how critical they are to her success and willingness to persevere. When asked, what do you think your family's expectations are for you? This student answered, they expect a lot because I was the one who started school [in the United States].... And I really appreciate that. If you expect something from somebody and you know they know you expect it from them they would really try to go into it.

Thus, for this student, her continued interest in computers is tied to her family's positive opinion of technology and their high expectations for her success in the field. She does not regard their control and expectations as intrusive but rather finds their input helpful, "so I know what to do and what not." By providing their daughter with clear direction and expectations of her success, this family is helping to encourage her to persevere in technology. These examples highlight conditions that encourage girls to consider a technical career pathway: family members who communicate enjoyment for their work, strong encouragement for a career in technology, and opportunities to see, hear, and learn about these careers.

Research indicates that many girls have limited career options and lack the information and guidance to make informed academic and career plans. Few of the girls we spoke with were encouraged to consider a career in technology, and few understood what a career in technology might encompass. It is our hope that by identifying the barriers that turn girls off to careers in technology, as well as the positive powerful impact that families can have, we can help broaden the career options of girls and increase the numbers interested in careers in technology.

Bibliography

Anker, R. and C. Hein, 'Why Third World Urban Employers Usually Prefer Men', *International Labour Review*, Vol. 124, No. I, Geneva, 1985.

Beech, C., *Women and Women into Information Technology*, a report by the British Computer Society, 1990.

Byrne, E., *Women in Science and Technology: The Institutional Ecology Approach*, Interim Research Report, Department of Education, University of Queensland, 1988.

Chew. S.B. and R. Chew, 'Information Technology as a Strategy Human Resource Development', in E.C.Y. Kuo, C.M. Loh and K.S. Raman, *Information Technology in Singapore Society: Trends, Policies and Applications*, Singapore University Press, 1990.

Davidson, M.J. and C.L. Cooper (eds), *Women and Information Technology*, Psychology and Productivity at Work Series, London, John Wiley and Sons, 1987.

Deakin, R., *Women and Computing: The Golden Opportunity*, London, Macmillan Press, 1984.

Eriksson, I.V., B.A. Kitchenham and K.G. Tijdens (eds), *Women, Work and Computerization: Understanding and Overcoming Bias in Work and Education*, Amsterdam, North Holland, 1991.

Faruqui, A.M., M.H.A. Hassan and G. Sandri (eds), *The Role of Women in the Development of Science and Technology in the Third World*, proceedings of the conference organized by CIDA and the Third World Academy of Sciences, Trieste, Italy, October, 1988.

Harrison, P. (1983), *The Third World Tomorrow*, NY, Pilgrim Press and Harmondsworth, Penguin

Irvine, J., 'Women into Information Technology', *Information Technology and Public Policy*, Vol. 8, No. 3, Summer, 1990.

Kluzer, S., *Computer Diffusion in Black Africa: A Preliminary Assessment*, unpublished paper, SPRU, University of Sussex, Brighton, UK, 1988.

Lim, G.K., 'Women's Participation in the Computer Industry in Singapore', in Ken Tijdens *et al.* (eds), *Women, Work and Computing: Forming New Alliances*, Amsterdam, North Holland, 1989.

Lovegrove, G. and B. Segal (eds), *Women into Computing: Selected Papers*, 1988-1990, London, Springer, 1991.

Mitter, S., 'Computer Aided Manufacturing and Women's Employment: a Global Critique of Post Fordism', in I.V. Eriksson, B.A. Kitchenham and K.G. Tijdens (eds). *Women, Work and Computerisation: Understanding and Overcoming Bias in Work and Education*, Amsterdam, North Holland, 1991.

Mumford, E., *Where are Tomorrow's Top Women Executives ?*, Manchester Business School Review, Vol. 4, No. 3, 1980.

Ng, C. (ed.), *Technology and Gender: Women's Work in Asia*, Women's Studies Unit, UPM and Malaysian Social Science Association, 1987.

Ng, C. and J. Othman, 'Information Technology, Gender and Employment in Malaysia', in S.C. Bhatnagar and M. Odedra (eds) *Social Implications of Computers in Developing Countries*, New Delhi, Tata-McGraw Hill, 1992.

Odedra, M., *Information Technology Transfer to Developing Countries: Case Studies from Kenya, Zambia and Zimbabwe*, unpublished Ph.D. thesis, London School of Economics, 1990a.

Odedra, M., 'Poor Management leads to Gross Underutilization', *Computer in Africa*, Vol. 4, No. 5, July, 1990b.

Parikh, I., *Women in Management: an Annotated Bibliography with Emphasis on Commonwealth Sources*, London, Commonwealth Secretariat, 1987.

Stamp, P., *Technology, Gender and Power in Africa*, Ottawa, international Development Research Centre, 1989.

Subramaniam, P.R., *The Future for Women in Information Technology*, M. Sc. dissertation, London School of Economics, 1991.

Tijdens, K., M. Jennings, I. Wagner and M. Weggelaar (eds), *Women Work and Computing: Forming New Alliances*, Amsterdam, North Holland, 1989.

Virgo, P., 'The Case for Women into Information Technology Campaign', *Information Technology and Public Policy*, Vol. 6, No. 3, Summer, 1988.

World Bank, *Sub-Saharan Africa: From Crisis to Sustainable Growth*, Washington DC, World Bank, 1989.

Wright, B.D. (ed.), *Women, Work and Technology: Transformations*, Chicago, University of Michigan Press, 1987.

Index

S

T

V

W